The American Journey

Reproducible Lesson Plans

D1242532

 **Glencoe McGraw-Hill**

New York, New York   Columbus, Ohio   Chicago, Illinois   Peoria, Illinois   Woodland Hills, California

Glencoe/McGraw-Hill

A Division of The **McGraw·Hill** *Companies*

Send all inquiries to:
Glencoe/McGraw-Hill
8787 Orion Place
Columbus, OH 43240

ISBN 0-07-825212-1

Printed in the United States of America

1 2 3 4 5 6 7 8 9 10 024 08 07 06 05 04 03 02

Table of Contents

To The Teacher

Guide to Using the *Reproducible Lesson Plans*

The *Reproducible Lesson Plans* are designed to help organize your instruction, shorten your preparation time, and provide you with a variety of teaching options. Each Lesson Plan is organized so that a teacher can easily identify all of the objectives, strategies, activities, and supplementary materials available (in the Teacher Wraparound Edition and Teacher Classroom Resources) for teaching that particular lesson. Each Lesson Plan also levels each activity listed (please see the key to ability levels below) and includes the expected range of completion time for each activity (for example, 10-15 minutes). The Lesson Plan for each section is presented in a convenient format that allows you to see, at a glance the resources and supplementary materials available for a particular lesson. The Lesson Plans can be easily reproduced and submitted to your supervisor or administrator to fulfill your district's specific curriculum and preparation requirements.

For your convenience, a blank column is provided in which you may list objectives. The right-hand column of each Lesson Plan begins with a list of the objectives that students should master after completing the section in the textbook. You may wish to point out these objectives to students and inform them that all review materials, as well as section quizzes, and chapter and unit tests, will be designed to test their mastery of these objectives.

The five-step teaching model that follows the objectives in the Lesson Plans is designed to actively involve students as they learn about history. These steps include the following:

Focus

This section presents various activities available to you to introduce students to the section. It includes, for example, references to activities in the Teacher Wraparound Edition as well as to the appropriate Daily Focus Skills Transparencies located in the Teacher Classroom Resources.

Teach

The Teach section of each Lesson Plan is divided into two parts—Guided Practice and Independent Practice. The Guided Practice category directs you to activities designed to be used with the entire class. In general, these are teacher-directed activities. The Guided Practice also directs you to other strategies included in the Teacher Wraparound Edition and the Teacher Classroom Resources.

The second category in the Teach section—Independent Practice—refers you to activities in which students take a more active role and assume more personal responsibility for mastering section objectives. These activities may include the appropriate activities in the Teacher Classroom Resources.

Assess

The Assess section of the Lesson Plans refers you to the assess activity in the Teacher Wraparound Edition as well as to the quizzes and tests that accompany the program. Alternately, if your class includes native-Spanish speakers, you may wish to have them use the Spanish chapter summary on audiocassette or CD as a review of the section or chapter. The Assess segment is designed to help you measure student mastery of the section objectives.

Reteaching and Enrichment

The Reteaching and Enrichment sections of the Lesson Plans refer you to the reteaching and enrichment activities in the Teacher Wraparound Edition as well as to the appropriate Reteaching Activity or Enrichment Activity in the Teacher Classroom Resources. In general, the reteaching activities are suitable for students who have not yet mastered the content of the section. The enrichment activities are designed to enrich and extend chapter content.

Close

The final section of each Lesson Plan—the Close section—refers you to the appropriate close activity in the Teacher Wraparound Edition.

KEY TO ABILITY LEVELS

Teaching strategies have been coded for varying learning styles and abilities.

L1 BASIC activities for all students
L2 AVERAGE activities for average to above-average students
L3 CHALLENGING activities for above-average students
ELL ENGLISH LANGUAGE LEARNER activities for native-Spanish speakers

Optional Resources Menu

Use these additional activities and multimedia products for *The American Journey* listed below to enhance your lessons and the study of history.

Teacher Planning and Support Resources

- Daily Lecture and Discussion Notes, TCR
- Inclusion for the Middle School Social Studies Classroom Strategies and Activities, TCR
- Presentation Plus! CD-ROM
- Reading in the Content Area, TCR
- TeacherWorks™ CD-ROM (Includes the Interactive Teacher Edition and Interactive Lesson Planner)
- Teaching Strategies for the American History Classroom (Including Block Scheduling Pacing Guides), TCR
- *The American Journey* Web site: www.taj.glencoe.com

Review and Reinforcement Resources

- Activity Workbook (and Teacher Annotated Edition), TCR
- Cause-and-Effect Transparencies with Teaching Strategies and Student Activities, TCR
- Critical Thinking Skills Activities, TCR
- Glencoe Skillbuilder Interactive Workbook CD-ROM, Level 1
- Interactive Student Edition CD-ROM
- Vocabulary PuzzleMaker CD-ROM

Application and Enrichment Resources

- American Crafts Hands-On Activities
- American Games Hands-On Activities
- American History Flash Cards
- American History Primary Source Document Library CD-ROM
- Citizenship Activities: History and Your Community, TCR
- Interpreting Political Cartoons, TCR
- Social Studies Guide to Using the Internet, TCR
- Supreme Court Case Studies, TCR
- *The American Journey* Video Program
- The Living Constitution (and Teacher Annotated Edition), TCR

Interdisciplinary Connections Resources

- American Art Prints (with Strategies and Activities)
- American Literature Readings, TCR
- American Music: Cultural Traditions
- American Music: Hits Through History
- Economics and History Activities, TCR
- Literature Connections
- Middle School Writer's Guidebook

Map and Geography Skills Resources

- Building Geography Skills for Life (workbook)
- Geography and History Activities, TCR
- National Geographic Society's U.S. Desk Maps
- Outline Map Resource Book, TCR
- Unit Map Overlay Transparencies with Teaching Strategies and Student Activities, TCR

Assessment and Evaluation Resources

- ExamView® Pro Testmaker CD-ROM
- Interactive Tutor Self-Assessment CD-ROM
- MindJogger Videoquiz
- Quizzes and Tests, TCR
- Standardized Test Practice Workbook (and Teacher Annotated Edition), TCR

Spanish Resources

- Spanish Guided Reading Activities
- Spanish Quizzes and Tests
- Spanish Reteaching Activities
- Spanish Summaries
- Spanish Take-Home Review Activities
- Spanish Vocabulary Activities
- The Declaration of Independence and United States Constitution Spanish Translations

Early Peoples

Section 1 *(pp. 16–19)*

LOCAL OBJECTIVES	TWE—Teacher Wraparound Edition TCR—Teacher Classroom Resources
	📁 Blackline Master ✍ Transparency 💿 CD-ROM 💽 DVD 📋 Poster
	🎵 Music Program 🎧 Audio Program 📼 Videocassette 🖱 Internet Resources

OBJECTIVES

1. Understand how the first people arrived in the Americas.

2. Cite the discovery that changed the lives of the early Native Americans.

FOCUS MENU	SUGGESTED TIME RANGES	SUGGESTED LEVELS
—— Daily Focus Skills Transparency 1–1, TCR ✍ 📁	5–10 minutes	L1
—— Preteaching Vocabulary, TWE, p. 16	5–10 minutes	All levels
—— History Online Chapter 1 Overview 🖱	15–20 minutes	All levels
—— Audio Program Chapter 1 🎧	20–30 minutes	All levels

TEACH MENU		
Guided Practice		
—— Time Line Activity, TWE, p. 15	10–15 minutes	All levels
—— Activity, TWE, p. 17	5–10 minutes	L1
—— Cooperative Learning Activity, TWE, p. 17	40–60 minutes	L2
—— Meeting Special Needs, TWE, p. 18	25–35 minutes	L1
—— Graphic Organizer Transparencies Strategies and Activities, TCR ✍ 📁	20–25 minutes	All levels
—— Why It Matters Chapter Transparency Strategy and Activity 1, TCR ✍ 📁	25–30 minutes	All levels
Independent Practice		
—— Guided Reading Activity 1–1, TCR 📁	15–20 minutes	ELL, L1
—— Reading and Study Skills Foldable, p. 15	10–15 minutes	All levels

ASSESS MENU		
Evaluate		
—— Section Quiz 1–1, TCR 📁	10–15 minutes	All levels
—— Interactive Tutor Self-Assessment CD-ROM 💿	25–30 minutes	All levels
—— ExamView® Pro Testmaker CD-ROM 💿	15–20 minutes	All levels
Reteach		
—— Reteaching Activity 1–1, TCR 📁	15–20 minutes	ELL, L1
—— Reading Essentials and Study Guide 1–1, TCR 📁	20–35 minutes	ELL, L1
Enrich		
—— Enrichment Activity 1–1, TCR 📁	10–15 minutes	L2, L3

CLOSE MENU		
—— Close, TWE, p. 19	10–15 minutes	All levels

See Optional Resources menu on page viii.

Grade _____ Class(es) _____ Date _____ M Tu W Th F

Teacher's Name _____ Date _____

Cities and Empires

Section 2 *(pp. 22–26)*

LOCAL OBJECTIVES	TWE—Teacher Wraparound Edition TCR—Teacher Classroom Resources
	📁 Blackline Master 🎚 Transparency 💿 CD-ROM 💿 DVD 📖 Poster
	🎵 Music Program 🎧 Audio Program 📼 Videocassette 🖱 Internet Resources

OBJECTIVES		
1. Describe why powerful empires arose in the Americas.		
2. Investigate how the people of each empire adapted to their environment.		

FOCUS MENU	**SUGGESTED TIME RANGES**	**SUGGESTED LEVELS**
____ Daily Focus Skills Transparency 1–2, TCR 🎚 📁	5–10 minutes	L1
____ Preteaching Vocabulary, TWE, p. 22	5–10 minutes	All levels
____ Audio Program Chapter 1 🎧	20–25 minutes	All levels

TEACH MENU		
Guided Practice		
____ Activity, TWE, p. 23	5–10 minutes	L1
____ Cooperative Learning Activity, TWE, p. 23	40–60 minutes	L2
____ Meeting Special Needs, TWE, p. 24	25–35 minutes	L1
____ Interdisciplinary Connections Activity, TWE, p. 25	20–30 minutes	ELL, L1
____ Graphic Organizer Transparency Strategy and Activity 1, TCR 🎚 📁	15–25 minutes	L2
Independent Practice		
____ Guided Reading Activity 1–2, TCR 📁	15–20 minutes	ELL, L1

ASSESS MENU		
Evaluate		
____ Section Quiz 1–2, TCR 📁	10–15 minutes	All levels
____ Interactive Tutor Self-Assessment CD-ROM 💿	20–30 minutes	All levels
____ ExamView® Pro Testmaker CD-ROM 💿	15–20 minutes	All levels
Reteach		
____ Reteaching Activity 1–2, TCR 📁	15–20 minutes	ELL, L1
____ Reading Essentials and Study Guide 1–2, TCR 📁	25–35 minutes	ELL, L1
Enrich		
____ Enrichment Activity 1–2, TCR 📁	10–15 minutes	L2, L3
____ Primary Source Reading 1, TCR 📁	20–30 minutes	All levels
____ Linking Past and Present Activity 1, TCR 📁	15–20 minutes	All levels

CLOSE MENU		
____ Close, TWE, p. 26	10–15 minutes	All levels

See Optional Resources menu on page viii.

North American Peoples

Section 3 *(pp. 28–33)*

LOCAL OBJECTIVES	TWE—Teacher Wraparound Edition TCR—Teacher Classroom Resources 📁 Blackline Master 📠 Transparency 💿 CD-ROM 💿 DVD 📔 Poster 🎵 Music Program 🔊 Audio Program 📼 Videocassette 🔗 Internet Resources

	OBJECTIVES **1.** Explore what early people lived in North America. **2.** Examine how different Native American groups adapted to their environments.		
	FOCUS MENU	**SUGGESTED TIME RANGES**	**SUGGESTED LEVELS**
	—— Daily Focus Skills Transparency 1–3, TCR 📠 📁	5–10 minutes	L1
	—— Vocabulary PuzzleMaker CD-ROM 💿	10–15 minutes	All levels
	—— Audio Program Chapter 1 🔊	20–30 minutes	All levels
	TEACH MENU **Guided Practice**		
	—— Activity, TWE, p. 29	5–10 minutes	ELL, L2
	—— Cooperative Learning Activity, TWE, p. 29	40–60 minutes	ELL, L2
	—— Meeting Special Needs, TWE, p. 30		
	—— Interdisciplinary Connections Activity, TWE, p. 31	25–35 minutes	L1
	—— Critical Thinking Activity, TWE, p. 32	20–30 minutes	L1
	—— Graphic Organizer Transparencies Strategies and Activities, TCR 📠 📁	20–25 minutes	L3
	—— History Online Activity 🔗	15–20 minutes	All levels
	—— American Art and Architecture 📠 📁	25–30 minutes	All levels
	Independent Practice		
	—— Guided Reading Activity 1–3, TCR 📁	20–30 minutes	ELL, L1
	—— Vocabulary Activity 1, TCR 📁	20–30 minutes	All levels
	—— Chapter Skills Activity 1, TCR 📁	20–30 minutes	All levels
	—— Critical Thinking Activity 1, TCR 📁	10–15 minutes	L2
	—— Geography and History Activity 1, TCR 📁	10–15 minutes	L1
	—— Time Line Activity 1, TCR 📁	15–20 minutes	L1
	ASSESS MENU **Evaluate**		
	—— Section Quiz 1–3, TCR 📁	10–15 minutes	All levels
	—— Performance Assessment Activity 1, TCR 📁	25–30 minutes	All levels
	—— Interactive Tutor Self-Assessment CD-ROM 💿	20–30 minutes	All levels
	—— ExamView® Pro Testmaker CD-ROM 💿	15–20 minutes	All levels
	Reteach		
	—— Reteaching Activity 1–3, TCR 📁	15–20 minutes	ELL, L1
	—— Reading Essentials and Study Guide 1–3, TCR 📁	25–35 minutes	ELL, L1
	—— Take-Home Review Activity 1, TCR 📁	10–15 minutes	All levels
	—— MindJogger Videoquiz, Chapter 1 💿 📼	20–25 minutes	All levels
	Enrich		
	—— Enrichment Activity 1–3, TCR 📁	10–15 minutes	L2, L3
	CLOSE MENU		
	—— Close, TWE, p. 33	10–15 minutes	All levels

See Optional Resources menu on page viii.

A Changing World

Section 1 *(pp. 38–42)*

LOCAL OBJECTIVES	TWE—Teacher Wraparound Edition TCR—Teacher Classroom Resources 📁 Blackline Master 🔖 Transparency 💿 CD-ROM 📀 DVD 📋 Poster 🎵 Music Program 🎧 Audio Program 📼 Videocassette 🖱 Internet Resources

	OBJECTIVES
	1. Examine how technology made long sea voyages possible.
	2. Explore the factors that allowed great civilizations in Africa to flourish.

	FOCUS MENU	**SUGGESTED TIME RANGES**	**SUGGESTED LEVELS**
	—— Daily Focus Skills Transparency 2–1, TCR 🔖 📁	5–10 minutes	L1
	—— Preteaching Vocabulary, TWE, p. 38	5–10 minutes	All levels
	—— History Online Chapter 2 Overview 🖱	15–20 minutes	All levels
	—— Audio Program Chapter 2 🎧	20–25 minutes	All levels

	TEACH MENU		
	Guided Practice		
	—— Time Line Activity, TWE, p. 37	5–10 minutes	All levels
	—— Activity, TWE, p. 39	5–10 minutes	L1
	—— Cooperative Learning Activity, TWE, p. 39	40–60 minutes	L2
	—— Meeting Special Needs, TWE, p. 40	25–35 minutes	L1
	—— Interdisciplinary Connections Activity, TWE, p. 41	20–30 minutes	ELL, L2
	—— Graphic Organizer Transparencies Strategies and Activities, TCR 🔖 📁	20–25 minutes	All levels
	Independent Practice		
	—— Guided Reading Activity 2–1, TCR 📁	15–20 minutes	ELL, L1
	—— Reading and Study Skills Foldable, p. 37	10–15 minutes	All levels

	ASSESS MENU		
	Evaluate		
	—— Section Quiz 2–1, TCR 📁	10–15 minutes	All levels
	—— Interactive Tutor Self-Assessment CD-ROM 💿	20–30 minutes	All levels
	—— ExamView® Pro Testmaker CD-ROM 💿	15–20 minutes	All levels
	—— History Online Activity 🖱	15–20 minutes	All levels
	Reteach		
	—— Reteaching Activity 2–1, TCR 📁	15–20 minutes	ELL, L1
	—— Reading Essentials and Study Guide 2–1, TCR 📁	25–35 minutes	ELL, L1
	Enrich		
	—— Enrichment Activity 2–1, TCR 📁	10–15 minutes	L2, L3

	CLOSE MENU		
	—— Close, TWE, p. 42	10–15 minutes	All levels

See Optional Resources menu on page viii.

Early Exploration

Section 2 (pp. 43–49)

LOCAL OBJECTIVES	TWE—Teacher Wraparound Edition TCR—Teacher Classroom Resources 📁 Blackline Master ✒ Transparency 💿 CD-ROM 💿 DVD 📕 Poster 🎌 Music Program 🎧 Audio Program 📼 Videocassette ✐ Internet Resources		
	OBJECTIVES **1.** Explain Portugal's leadership roles in exploration. **2.** Understand Columbus's plan for sailing to Asia.		
	FOCUS MENU	**SUGGESTED TIME RANGES**	**SUGGESTED LEVELS**
	——— Daily Focus Skills Transparency 2–2, TCR ✒ 📁	5–10 minutes	L1
	——— Preteaching Vocabulary, TWE, p. 43	5–10 minutes	All levels
	——— Audio Program Chapter 2 🎧	20–25 minutes	All levels
	TEACH MENU **Guided Practice**		
	——— Activity, TWE, p. 44	5–10 minutes	L2
	——— Cooperative Learning Activity, TWE, p. 44	40–60 minutes	L1
	——— Meeting Special Needs, TWE, p. 45	25–35 minutes	L1
	——— Interdisciplinary Connections Activity, TWE, p. 46	20–30 minutes	ELL, L1
	——— Critical Thinking Activity, TWE, p. 47	20–35 minutes	L2
	——— Extending the Content, TWE, p. 48	5–10 minutes	All levels
	——— Graphic Organizer Transparencies Strategies and Activities, TCR ✒ 📁	20–25 minutes	All levels
	Independent Practice		
	——— Guided Reading Activity 2–2, TCR 📁	15–20 minutes	ELL, L1
	ASSESS MENU **Evaluate**		
	——— Section Quiz 2–2, TCR 📁	10–15 minutes	All levels
	——— Interactive Tutor Self-Assessment CD-ROM 💿	20–30 minutes	All levels
	——— ExamView® Pro Testmaker CD-ROM 💿	15–20 minutes	All levels
	Reteach		
	——— Reteaching Activity 2–2, TCR 📁	15–20 minutes	ELL, L1
	——— Reading Essentials and Study Guide 2–2, TCR 📁	25–35 minutes	ELL, L1
	Enrich		
	——— Enrichment Activity 2–2, TCR 📁	10–15 minutes	L2, L3
	CLOSE MENU		
	——— Close, TWE, p. 49	10–15 minutes	All levels

See Optional Resources menu on page viii.

Spain in America

Section 3 *(pp. 51–55)*

LOCAL OBJECTIVES	TWE—Teacher Wraparound Edition TCR—Teacher Classroom Resources 📁 Blackline Master 🖌 Transparency 💿 CD-ROM 💿 DVD 📋 Poster 🏁 Music Program 🎧 Audio Program 📼 Videocassette 🖱 Internet Resources		
	OBJECTIVES **1.** Evaluate the decline of the Aztec and Inca empires in the Americas. **2.** Explore how Spain governed its empire in the Americas.		
	FOCUS MENU	**SUGGESTED TIME RANGES**	**SUGGESTED LEVELS**
	—— Daily Focus Skills Transparency 2–3, TCR 🖌 📁	5–10 minutes	L1
	—— Preteaching Vocabulary, TWE, p. 51	5–10 minutes	All levels
	—— Audio Program Chapter 2 🎧	20–25 minutes	All levels
	TEACH MENU **Guided Practice**		
	—— Activity, TWE, p. 52	5–10 minutes	ELL, L2
	—— Cooperative Learning Activity, TWE, p. 52	40–60 minutes	L3
	—— Meeting Special Needs, TWE, p. 53	25–35 minutes	L1
	—— Interdisciplinary Connections Activity, TWE, p. 54	20–30 minutes	ELL, L2
	—— Graphic Organizer Transparency Strategy and Activity 2, TCR 🖌 📁	15–25 minutes	L2
	—— American Art and Architecture 🖌 📁	25–30 minutes	All levels
	Independent Practice		
	—— Guided Reading Activity 2–3, TCR 📁	15–20 minutes	ELL, L1
	ASSESS MENU **Evaluate**		
	—— Section Quiz 2-3, TCR 📁	10–15 minutes	All levels
	—— Interactive Tutor Self-Assessment CD-ROM 💿	20–30 minutes	All levels
	—— ExamView® Pro Testmaker CD-ROM 💿	15–20 minutes	All levels
	Reteach		
	—— Reteaching Activity 2–3, TCR 📁	15–20 minutes	ELL, L1
	—— Reading Essentials and Study Guide 2–3, TCR 📁	25–35 minutes	ELL, L1
	Enrich		
	—— Enrichment Activity 2–3, TCR 📁	10–15 minutes	L2, L3
	—— Linking Past and Present, Activity 2, TCR 📁	15–20 minutes	All levels
	CLOSE MENU		
	—— Close, TWE, p. 55	10–15 minutes	All levels

See Optional Resources menu on page viii.

Exploring North America

Section 4 *(pp. 58–62)*

LOCAL OBJECTIVES	TWE—Teacher Wraparound Edition TCR—Teacher Classroom Resources 📁 Blackline Master 🖊 Transparency 💿 CD-ROM 💿 DVD 📗 Poster 🏁 Music Program 🎧 Audio Program 📼 Videocassette 🖱 Internet Resources

OBJECTIVES
1. Explain how the Protestant Reformation affected North America.
2. Evaluate why the activities of early traders encouraged exploration.

FOCUS MENU	**SUGGESTED TIME RANGES**	**SUGGESTED LEVELS**
____ Daily Focus Skills Transparency 2–4, TCR 🖊 📁	5–10 minutes	L1
____ Vocabulary PuzzleMaker CD-ROM 💿	10–15 minutes	All levels
____ Audio Program Chapter 2 🎧	20–25 minutes	All levels

TEACH MENU
Guided Practice

____ Activity, TWE, p. 59	5–10 minutes	L1
____ Cooperative Learning Activity, TWE, p. 59	40–60 minutes	L2
____ Meeting Special Needs, TWE, p. 60	25–35 minutes	L1
____ Interdisciplinary Connections Activity, TWE, p. 61	20–30 minutes	L2
____ Graphic Organizer Transparencies Strategies and Activities, TCR 🖊 📁	20–25 minutes	All levels
____ Why It Matters Chapter Transparency Strategy and Activity 2, TCR 🖊 📁	25–30 minutes	All levels

Independent Practice

____ Guided Reading Activity 2–4, TCR 📁	15–20 minutes	All levels
____ Vocabulary Activity 2, TCR 📁	20–30 minutes	All levels
____ Chapter Skills Activity 2, TCR 📁	20–30 minutes	All levels
____ Critical Thinking Activity 2, TCR 📁	10–15 minutes	L2
____ Geography and History Activity 2, TCR 📁	10–15 minutes	L1
____ Time Line Activity 2, TCR 📁	10–15 minutes	All levels

ASSESS MENU
Evaluate

____ Section Quiz 2–4, TCR 📁	10–15 minutes	All levels
____ Performance Assessment Activity 2, TCR 📁	25–30 minutes	All levels
____ Interactive Tutor Self-Assessment CD-ROM 💿	20–30 minutes	All levels
____ ExamView® Pro Testmaker CD-ROM 💿	15–20 minutes	All levels

Reteach

____ Reteaching Activity 2–4, TCR 📁	15–20 minutes	ELL, L1
____ Reading Essentials and Study Guide 2–4, TCR 📁	25–35 minutes	ELL, L1
____ Take-Home Review Activity 2, TCR 📁	10–15 minutes	All levels
____ MindJogger Videoquiz, Chapter 2 💿 📼	20–25 minutes	All levels

Enrich

____ Enrichment Activity 2–4, TCR 📁	10–15 minutes	L2, L3
____ Primary Source Reading 2, TCR 📁	20–30 minutes	All levels

CLOSE MENU

____ Close, TWE, p. 62	10–15 minutes	All levels

See Optional Resources menu on page viii.

Early English Settlements

Section 1 *(pp. 70–73)*

LOCAL OBJECTIVES	TWE—Teacher Wraparound Edition TCR—Teacher Classroom Resources		
	📁 Blackline Master ✒ Transparency ⊙ CD-ROM ⊙ DVD ▯ Poster		
	🎵 Music Program 🎧 Audio Program ▭ Videocassette ➛ Internet Resources		

OBJECTIVES

1. Identify the crop that saved the people of Jamestown.
2. Explain how the colonists received political rights.

FOCUS MENU	SUGGESTED TIME RANGES	SUGGESTED LEVELS
—— Daily Focus Skills Transparency 3–1, TCR ✒ 📁	5–10 minutes	L1
—— Preteaching Vocabulary, TWE, p. 70	5–10 minutes	All levels
—— History Online Chapter 3 Overview ➛	15–20 minutes	All levels
—— Audio Program Chapter 3 🎧	20–25 minutes	All levels

TEACH MENU		
Guided Practice		
—— Time Line Activity, TWE, p. 69	5–10 minutes	L2
—— Activity, TWE, p. 71	5–10 minutes	L1
—— Cooperative Learning Activity, TWE, p. 71	40–60 minutes	L2
—— Meeting Special Needs, TWE, p. 72	25–35 minutes	L1
—— Graphic Organizer Transparencies Strategies and Activities, TCR ✒ 📁	20–25 minutes	All levels
Independent Practice		
—— Guided Reading Activity 3–1, TCR 📁	15–20 minutes	ELL, L1
—— Reading and Study Skills Foldable, p. 69	10–15 minutes	All levels

ASSESS MENU		
Evaluate		
—— Section Quiz 3-1, TCR 📁	10–15 minutes	All levels
—— Interactive Tutor Self-Assessment CD-ROM ⊙	20–30 minutes	All levels
—— ExamView® Pro Testmaker CD-ROM ⊙	15–20 minutes	All levels
Reteach		
—— Reteaching Activity 3–1, TCR 📁	15–20 minutes	ELL, L1
—— Reading Essentials and Study Guide 3–1, TCR 📁	25–35 minutes	ELL, L1
Enrich		
—— Enrichment Activity 3–1, TCR 📁	10–15 minutes	L2, L3
—— Linking Past and Present Activity 3, TCR 📁	15–20 minutes	All levels

CLOSE MENU		
—— Close, TWE, p. 73	10–15 minutes	All levels

See Optional Resources menu on page viii.

New England Colonies
Section 2 *(pp. 76–80)*

LOCAL OBJECTIVES	TWE—Teacher Wraparound Edition 📁 Blackline Master 🖉 Transparency 🌀 Music Program 🔊 Audio Program	TCR—Teacher Classroom Resources 💿 CD-ROM 💿 DVD 📖 Poster 📼 Videocassette ⌁ Internet Resources

OBJECTIVES

1. Explain why the Pilgrims and the Puritans came to America.

2. Describe how the Connecticut, Rhode Island, and New Hampshire colonies began.

	FOCUS MENU	**SUGGESTED TIME RANGES**	**SUGGESTED LEVELS**
	—— Daily Focus Skills Transparency 3–2, TCR 🖉 📁	5–10 minutes	L1
	—— Preteaching Vocabulary, TWE, p. 76	5–10 minutes	All levels
	—— Audio Program Chapter 3 🔊	20–25 minutes	All levels

	TEACH MENU		
	Guided Practice		
	—— Activity, TWE, p. 77	5–10 minutes	ELL, L1
	—— Cooperative Learning Activity, TWE, p. 77	40–60 minutes	L1
	—— Meeting Special Needs, TWE, p. 78	25–35 minutes	L1
	—— Interdisciplinary Connections Activity, TWE, p. 79	20–30 minutes	L2
	—— Graphic Organizer Transparency Strategy and Activity 3, TCR 🖉 📁	15–25 minutes	L2
	Independent Practice		
	—— Guided Reading Activity 3–2, TCR 📁	15–20 minutes	ELL, L1

	ASSESS MENU		
	Evaluate		
	—— Section Quiz 3–2, TCR 📁	10–15 minutes	All levels
	—— Interactive Tutor Self-Assessment CD-ROM 💿	20–30 minutes	All levels
	—— ExamView® Pro Testmaker CD-ROM 💿	15–20 minutes	All levels
	—— History Online Activity ⌁	15–20 minutes	All levels
	Reteach		
	—— Reteaching Activity 3–2, TCR 📁	15–20 minutes	ELL, L1
	—— Reading Essentials and Study Guide 3–2, TCR 📁	25–35 minutes	ELL, L1
	Enrich		
	—— Enrichment Activity 3–2, TCR 📁	10–15 minutes	L2, L3
	—— Primary Source Reading 3, TCR 📁	20–30 minutes	All levels

	CLOSE MENU		
	—— Close, TWE, p. 80	10–15 minutes	All levels

See Optional Resources menu on page viii.

Middle Colonies

Section 3 *(pp. 82–85)*

LOCAL OBJECTIVES	TWE—Teacher Wraparound Edition TCR—Teacher Classroom Resources		
	📁 Blackline Master ✒ Transparency 💿 CD-ROM 💿 DVD 📙 Poster		
	🎵 Music Program 🔊 Audio Program 📼 Videocassette 🖱 Internet Resources		

		SUGGESTED TIME RANGES	SUGGESTED LEVELS
	OBJECTIVES **1.** Explain why the Middle Colonies had the most diverse populations in colonial America. **2.** Identify America's first town planner.		
	FOCUS MENU		
	_____ Daily Focus Skills Transparency 3–3, TCR ✒ 📁	5–10 minutes	L1
	_____ Preteaching Vocabulary, TWE, p. 82	5–10 minutes	All levels
	_____ Audio Program Chapter 3 🔊	20–25 minutes	All levels
	TEACH MENU **Guided Practice**		
	_____ Activity, TWE, p. 83	5–10 minutes	ELL, L1
	_____ Cooperative Learning Activity, TWE, p. 83	40–60 minutes	L1
	_____ Meeting Special Needs, TWE, p. 84	25–35 minutes	L1
	_____ Graphic Organizer Transparencies Strategies and Activities, TCR ✒ 📁	20–25 minutes	All levels
	Independent Practice		
	_____ Guided Reading Activity 3–3, TCR 📁	15–20 minutes	ELL. L1
	_____ Vocabulary Activity 3, TCR 📁	20–30 minutes	All levels
	ASSESS MENU **Evaluate**		
	_____ Section Quiz 3–3, TCR 📁	10–15 minutes	All levels
	_____ Interactive Tutor Self-Assessment CD-ROM 💿	20–30 minutes	All levels
	_____ ExamView® Pro Testmaker CD-ROM 💿	15–20 minutes	All levels
	Reteach		
	_____ Reteaching Activity 3–3, TCR 📁	15–20 minutes	ELL, L1
	_____ Reading Essentials and Study Guide 3–3, TCR 📁	25–35 minutes	ELL, L1
	Enrich		
	_____ Enrichment Activity 3–3, TCR 📁	10–15 minutes	L2, L3
	CLOSE MENU		
	_____ Close, TWE, p. 85	10–15 minutes	All levels

See Optional Resources menu on page viii.

Southern Colonies

Section 4 *(pp. 86–93)*

LOCAL OBJECTIVES	TWE—Teacher Wraparound Edition TCR—Teacher Classroom Resources 📁 Blackline Master 🔥 Transparency 💿 CD-ROM 💿 DVD 🖼 Poster 🎵 Music Program 🔊 Audio Program 📼 Videocassette 🌐 Internet Resources		
	OBJECTIVES **1.** Understand why the Southern Colonies were established. **2.** Compare and contrast France's colony in North America with the English colonies.		
	FOCUS MENU	**SUGGESTED TIME RANGES**	**SUGGESTED LEVELS**
	—— Daily Focus Skills Transparency 3–4, TCR 🔥 📁	5–10 minutes	L1
	—— Vocabulary PuzzleMaker CD-ROM 💿	10–15 minutes	All levels
	TEACH MENU **Guided Practice**		
	—— Activity, TWE, p. 87	5–10 minutes	L1
	—— Cooperative Learning Activity, TWE, p. 87	40–60 minutes	L2
	—— Meeting Special Needs, TWE, p. 88	25–35 minutes	L1
	—— Interdisciplinary Connections Activity, TWE, p. 89	20–30 minutes	L2
	—— Critical Thinking Activity, TWE, p. 90	20–25 minutes	L2
	—— Extending the Content, TWE, p. 91	5–10 minutes	All levels
	—— Extending the Content, TWE, p. 92	5–10 minutes	All levels
	—— Graphic Organizer Transparencies Strategies and Activities, TCR 🔥 📁	20–25 minutes	All levels
	—— Why It Matters Chapter Transparency Strategy and Activity 3, TCR 🔥 📁	25–30 minutes 25–30 minutes	All levels All levels
	Independent Practice		
	—— Guided Reading Activity 3–4, TCR 📁	15–20 minutes	All levels
	—— Vocabulary Activity 3, TCR 📁	20–30 minutes	All levels
	—— Chapter Skills Activity 3, TCR 📁	20–30 minutes	All levels
	—— Critical Thinking Activity 3, TCR 📁	15–20 minutes	L2
	—— Geography and History Activity 3, TCR 📁	10–15 minutes	L1
	—— Time Line Activity 3, TCR 📁	15–20 minutes	L1
	ASSESS MENU **Evaluate**		
	—— Section Quiz 3–4, TCR 📁	10–15 minutes	All levels
	—— Performance Assessment Activity 3, TCR 📁	25–30 minutes	All levels
	—— Interactive Tutor Self-Assessment CD-ROM 💿	20–30 minutes	All levels
	—— ExamView® Pro Testmaker CD-ROM 💿	15–20 minutes	All levels
	Reteach		
	—— Reteaching Activity 3–4, TCR 📁	15–20 minutes	ELL, L1
	—— Reading Essentials and Study Guide 3–4, TCR 📁	25–35 minutes	ELL, L1
	—— Take-Home Review Activity 3, TCR 📁	10–15 minutes	All levels
	—— MindJogger Videoquiz, Chapter 3 💿 📼	20–25 minutes	All levels
	Enrich		
	—— Enrichment Activity 3–4, TCR 📁	10–15 minutes	L2, L3
	CLOSE MENU —— Close, TWE, p. 93	10–15 minutes	All levels

See Optional Resources menu on page viii.

Grade _____ Class(es) _____ Date _____ M Tu W Th F

Teacher's Name _____ Date _____

Life in the Colonies
Section 1 *(pp. 100–106)*

LOCAL OBJECTIVES	TWE—Teacher Wraparound Edition 　　　TCR—Teacher Classroom Resources
	📁 Blackline Master 　🎙 Transparency 　💿 CD-ROM 　　💿 DVD 　　💻 Poster
	🎵 Music Program 　🔊 Audio Program 　📼 Videocassette 　🖰 Internet Resources

	OBJECTIVES
	1. Define the triangular trade and explain how it affected American society.
	2. Understand how the regions in the colonies differed from one another.
	3. Understand why the use of enslaved workers increased in the colonies.

	FOCUS MENU	**SUGGESTED TIME RANGES**	**SUGGESTED LEVELS**
	____ Daily Focus Skills Transparency 4–1, TCR 🎙 📁	5–10 minutes	L1
	____ History Online Chapter 4 Overview 🖰	15–20 minutes	All levels
	____ Preteaching Vocabulary, TWE, p. 100	5–10 minutes	All levels
	____ Audio Program Chapter 4 🔊	20–25 minutes	All levels

	TEACH MENU		
	Guided Practice		
	____ Time Line Activity, TWE, p. 99	10–15 minutes	All levels
	____ Activity, TWE, p. 101	5–10 minutes	L1
	____ Cooperative Learning Activity, TWE, p. 101	40–60 minutes	ELL, L1
	____ Meeting Special Needs, TWE, p. 102	25–35 minutes	L1
	____ Interdisciplinary Connections Activity, TWE, p. 103	20–30 minutes	ELL, L2
	____ Critical Thinking Activity, TWE, p. 104	20–25 minutes	L2
	____ Extending the Content, TWE, p. 105	5–10 minutes	All levels
	____ Graphic Organizer Transparency Strategy and Activity 4, TCR 🎙 📁	15–25 minutes	L2
	Independent Practice		
	____ Guided Reading Activity 4–1, TCR 📁	15–20 minutes	ELL, L1
	____ Reading and Study Skills Foldable, p. 99	10–15 minutes	All levels

	ASSESS MENU		
	Evaluate		
	____ Section Quiz 4–1, TCR 📁	10–15 minutes	All levels
	____ Interactive Tutor Self-Assessment CD-ROM 💿	20–30 minutes	All levels
	____ ExamView® Pro Testmaker p CD-ROM 💿	15–20 minutes	All levels
	Reteach		
	____ Reteaching Activity 4–1, TCR 📁	15–20 minutes	ELL, L1
	____ Reading Essentials and Study Guide 4–1, TCR 📁	25–35 minutes	ELL, L1
	Enrich		
	____ Enrichment Activity 4–1, TCR 📁	10–15 minutes	L2, L3
	____ Primary Source Reading 4, TCR 📁	20–30 minutes	All levels

	CLOSE MENU		
	____ Close, TWE, p. 106	10–15 minutes	All levels

See Optional Resources menu on page viii.

Grade _____ Class(es) _____ Date _____ M Tu W Th F

Teacher's Name _____ Date _____

Government, Religion, and Culture   Section 2 *(pp. 108–113)*

LOCAL OBJECTIVES	TWE—Teacher Wraparound Edition TCR—Teacher Classroom Resources 📁 Blackline Master 🖌 Transparency 💿 CD-ROM 📀 DVD 📔 Poster 🎵 Music Program 🎧 Audio Program 📼 Videocassette 🖱 Internet Resources

<table>
<tr><td rowspan="3"></td><td colspan="3">OBJECTIVES
1. Understand why the Navigation Acts angered the colonies.
2. Identify the people who had the right to vote in colonial legislatures.</td></tr>
<tr><td>FOCUS MENU</td><td>SUGGESTED TIME RANGES</td><td>SUGGESTED LEVELS</td></tr>
<tr>
<td>—— Daily Focus Skills Transparency 4–2, TCR 🖌 📁
—— Preteaching Vocabulary, TWE, p. 108
—— Audio Program Chapter 4 🎧</td>
<td>5–10 minutes
5–10 minutes
20–25 minutes</td>
<td>L1
All levels
All levels</td>
</tr>
<tr>
<td></td>
<td>TEACH MENU
Guided Practice
—— Activity, TWE, p. 109
—— Cooperative Learning Activity, TWE, p. 109
—— Meeting Special Needs, TWE, p. 110
—— Interdisciplinary Connections Activity, TWE, p. 111
—— Critical Thinking Activity, TWE, p. 112
—— Graphic Organizer Transparencies
Strategies and Activities, TCR 🖌 📁
—— Why It Matters Chapter Transparency
Strategy and Activity 4, TCR 🖌 📁
Independent Practice
—— Guided Reading Activity 4–2, TCR 📁</td>
<td>

5–10 minutes
40–60 minutes
25–35 minutes
20–30 minutes
20–25 minutes
20–25 minutes

25–30 minutes

15–20 minutes</td>
<td>

ELL, L1
ELL, L1
L1
ELL, L1
L2
All levels

All levels

ELL, L1</td>
</tr>
<tr>
<td></td>
<td>ASSESS MENU
Evaluate
—— Section Quiz 4–2, TCR 📁
—— Interactive Tutor Self-Assessment CD-ROM 💿
—— ExamView® Pro Testmaker CD-ROM 💿
Reteach
—— Reteaching Activity 4–2, TCR 📁
—— Reading Essentials and Study Guide 4–2, TCR 📁
Enrich
—— Enrichment Activity 4–2, TCR 📁
—— Linking Past and Present Activity 4, TCR 📁</td>
<td>

10–15 minutes
20–30 minutes
15–20 minutes

15–20 minutes
25–35 minutes

10–15 minutes
15–20 minutes</td>
<td>

All levels
All levels
All levels

ELL, L1
ELL, L1

L2, L3
All levels</td>
</tr>
<tr>
<td></td>
<td>CLOSE MENU
—— Close, TWE, p. 113</td>
<td>
10–15 minutes</td>
<td>
All levels</td>
</tr>
</table>

See Optional Resources menu on page viii.

Grade _____ Class(es) _____ Date _____ M Tu W Th F

Teacher's Name _____ Date _____

France and Britain Clash   Section 3 (pp. 116–119)

LOCAL OBJECTIVES	TWE—Teacher Wraparound Edition TCR—Teacher Classroom Resources		

TWE—Teacher Wraparound Edition   TCR—Teacher Classroom Resources
📁 Blackline Master   ⚒ Transparency   ⊚ CD-ROM   ⊙ DVD   📗 Poster
🏁 Music Program   ◉ Audio Program   📼 Videocassette   ☞ Internet Resources

OBJECTIVES
1. Explain how wars in Europe spread to the American colonies.
2. Understand the purpose of the Albany Plan of Union.

FOCUS MENU	SUGGESTED TIME RANGES	SUGGESTED LEVELS
—— Daily Focus Skills Transparency 4–3, TCR ⚒ 📁	5–10 minutes	L1
—— Preteaching Vocabulary, TWE, p. 116	5–10 minutes	All levels
—— Audio Program Chapter 4 ◉	20–25 minutes	All levels

TEACH MENU

Guided Practice

—— Activity, TWE, p. 117	5–10 minutes	L1
—— Cooperative Learning Activity, TWE, p. 117	40–60 minutes	L2
—— Meeting Special Needs, TWE, p. 118	25–35 minutes	L1
—— Graphic Organizer Transparencies Strategies and Activities, TCR ⚒ 📁	20–25 minutes	All levels

Independent Practice

—— Guided Reading Activity 4–3, TCR 📁	15–20 minutes	ELL, L1

ASSESS MENU

Evaluate

—— Section Quiz 4–3, TCR 📁	10–15 minutes	All levels
—— Interactive Tutor Self-Assessment CD-ROM ⊚	20–30 minutes	All levels
—— ExamView® Pro Testmaker CD-ROM ⊚	15–20 minutes	All levels

Reteach

—— Reteaching Activity 4–3, TCR 📁	15–20 minutes	ELL, L1
—— Reading Essentials and Study Guide 4–3, TCR 📁	25–35 minutes	ELL, L1

Enrich

—— Enrichment Activity 4–3, TCR 📁	10–15 minutes	L2, L3

CLOSE MENU

—— Close, TWE, p. 119	10–15 minutes	All levels

See Optional Resources menu on page viii.

The French and Indian War   Section 4 (pp. 121–125)

LOCAL OBJECTIVES	TWE—Teacher Wraparound Edition TCR—Teacher Classroom Resources
	📁 Blackline Master 🖐 Transparency 🔘 CD-ROM 🔘 DVD 📙 Poster
	🎵 Music Program 🔊 Audio Program 📼 Videocassette 🔌 Internet Resources

	OBJECTIVES
	1. Explain how British fortunes improved after William Pitt took over direction of the war.
	2. Describe how Chief Pontiac united his people to fight for their land.

	FOCUS MENU	SUGGESTED TIME RANGES	SUGGESTED LEVELS
	—— Daily Focus Skills Transparency 4–4, TCR 🖐 📁	5–10 minutes	L1
	—— Vocabulary PuzzleMaker CD-ROM 🔘	10–15 minutes	All levels
	—— Audio Program Chapter 4 🔊	20–25 minutes	All levels

	TEACH MENU		
	Guided Practice		
	—— Activity, TWE, p. 122	5–10 minutes	ELL, L2
	—— Cooperative Learning Activity, TWE, p. 122	40–60 minutes	L3
	—— Meeting Special Needs, TWE, p. 123	25–35 minutes	L1
	—— Interdisciplinary Connections Activity, TWE, p. 124	20–30 minutes	L3
	—— Graphic Organizer Transparencies Strategies and Activities, TCR 🖐 📁	20–25 minutes	All levels
	Independent Practice		
	—— Guided Reading Activity 4–4, TCR 📁	15–20 minutes	All levels
	—— Vocabulary Activity 4, TCR 📁	20–30 minutes	All levels
	—— Chapter Skills Activity 4, TCR 📁	20–30 minutes	L1
	—— Critical Thinking Activity 4, TCR 📁	15–20 minutes	L1
	—— Geography and History Activity 4, TCR 📁	10–15 minutes	L1
	—— Time Line Activity 4, TCR 📁	15–20 minutes	All levels

	ASSESS MENU		
	Evaluate		
	—— Section Quiz 4–4, TCR 📁	10–15 minutes	All levels
	—— Performance Assessment Activity 4, TCR 📁	25–30 minutes	All levels
	—— Interactive Tutor Self-Assessment CD-ROM 🔘	20–30 minutes	All levels
	—— ExamView® Pro Testmaker CD-ROM 🔘	15–20 minutes	All levels
	—— History Online Activity 🔌	15–20 minutes	All levels
	Reteach		
	—— Reteaching Activity 4–4, TCR 📁	15–20 minutes	ELL, L1
	—— Reading Essentials and Study Guide 4–4, TCR 📁	25–35 minutes	ELL, L1
	—— Take-Home Review Activity 4, TCR 📁	10–15 minutes	All levels
	—— MindJogger Videoquiz, Chapter 4 🔘 📼	20–25 minutes	All levels
	Enrich		
	—— Enrichment Activity 4–4, TCR 📁	10–15 minutes	L2, L3

	CLOSE MENU		
	—— Close, TWE, p. 125	10–15 minutes	All levels

See Optional Resources menu on page viii.

Taxation without Representation   Section 1 *(pp. 132–135)*

LOCAL OBJECTIVES	TWE—Teacher Wraparound Edition TCR—Teacher Classroom Resources
	📁 Blackline Master ✎ Transparency 💿 CD-ROM 💿 DVD 📖 Poster
	🏳 Music Program 🎧 Audio Program 📼 Videocassette ⌐ Internet Resources

	OBJECTIVES **1.** Describe why the British had problems in North America after the French and Indian War. **2.** Explain how the colonists responded to unpopular British laws.

		SUGGESTED TIME RANGES	SUGGESTED LEVELS
	FOCUS MENU		
	____ Daily Focus Skills Transparency 5–1, TCR ✎ 📁	5–10 minutes	L1
	____ Preteaching Vocabulary, TWE, p. 132	5–10 minutes	All levels
	____ History Online Chapter 5 Overview ⌐	15–20 minutes	All levels
	____ Audio Program Chapter 5 🎧	20–25 minutes	All levels
	TEACH MENU		
	Guided Practice		
	____ Time Line Activity, TWE, p. 131	5–10 minutes	All levels
	____ Activity, TWE, p. 133	5–10 minutes	L1
	____ Cooperative Learning Activity, TWE, p. 133	40–60 minutes	L1
	____ Meeting Special Needs, TWE, p. 134	25–35 minutes	L1
	____ Graphic Organizer Transparency Strategy and Activity 5, TCR ✎ 📁	15–20 minutes	L2
	Independent Practice		
	____ Guided Reading Activity 5–1, TCR 📁	15–20 minutes	ELL, L1
	____ Reading and Study Skills Foldable, p. 131	10–15 minutes	All levels
	ASSESS MENU		
	Evaluate		
	____ Section Quiz 5–1, TCR 📁	10–15 minutes	All levels
	____ Interactive Tutor Self-Assessment CD-ROM 💿	20–30 minutes	All levels
	____ ExamView® Pro Testmaker CD-ROM 💿	15–20 minutes	All levels
	Reteach		
	____ Reteaching Activity 5-1, TCR 📁	15–20 minutes	ELL, L1
	____ Reading Essentials and Study Guide 5–1, TCR 📁	25–35 minutes	ELL, L1
	Enrich		
	____ Enrichment Activity 5–1, TCR 📁	10–15 minutes	L2, L3
	CLOSE MENU		
	____ Close, TWE, p. 135	10–15 minutes	All levels

See Optional Resources menu on page viii.

Building Colonial Unity   Section 2 *(pp. 136–139)*

LOCAL OBJECTIVES	TWE—Teacher Wraparound Edition TCR—Teacher Classroom Resources 📁 Blackline Master 📌 Transparency 💿 CD-ROM 💿 DVD 🖼 Poster 🎵 Music Program 🎧 Audio Program 📼 Videocassette 🔗 Internet Resources		
	OBJECTIVES **1.** Identify the causes of the Boston Massacre. **2.** Explain how Britain tried to maintain its control over the colonies.		
	FOCUS MENU	**SUGGESTED TIME RANGES**	**SUGGESTED LEVELS**
	—— Daily Focus Skills Transparency 5–2, TCR 📌 📁	5–10 minutes	L1
	—— Preteaching Vocabulary, TWE, p. 136	5–10 minutes	All levels
	—— Audio Program Chapter 5 🎧	20–25 minutes	All levels
	TEACH MENU **Guided Practice**		
	—— Activity, TWE, p. 137	5–10 minutes	L1
	—— Cooperative Learning Activity, TWE, p. 137	40–60 minutes	ELL, L1
	—— Meeting Special Needs, TWE, p. 138	25–35 minutes	L1
	—— Graphic Organizer Transparencies Strategies and Activities, TCR 📌 📁	20–25 minutes	All levels
	Independent Practice		
	—— Guided Reading Activity 5–2, TCR 📁	15–20 minutes	ELL, L1
	ASSESS MENU **Evaluate**		
	—— Section Quiz 5–2, TCR 📁	10–15 minutes	All levels
	—— Interactive Tutor Self-Assessment CD-ROM 💿	20–30 minutes	All levels
	—— ExamView® Pro Testmaker CD-ROM 💿	15–20 minutes	All levels
	Reteach		
	—— Reteaching Activity 5–2, TCR 📁	15–20 minutes	ELL, L1
	—— Reading Essentials and Study Guide 5-2, TCR 📁	25–35 minutes	ELL, L1
	Enrich		
	—— Enrichment Activity 5–2, TCR 📁	10–15 minutes	L2, L3
	—— Linking Past and Present Activity 5, TCR 📁	15–20 minutes	All levels
	CLOSE MENU —— Close, TWE, p. 139	10–15 minutes	All levels

See Optional Resources menu on page viii.

A Call to Arms

Section 3 (pp. 141–145)

LOCAL OBJECTIVES	TWE—Teacher Wraparound Edition TCR—Teacher Classroom Resources
	📁 Blackline Master ✒ Transparency ⦿ CD-ROM ⦿ DVD 📙 Poster
	🎵 Music Program 🔊 Audio Program 📼 Videocassette 🖱 Internet Resources

OBJECTIVES

1. Identify the events that took place at the Continental Congress.

2. Describe the early skirmishes of the American Revolution.

	FOCUS MENU	SUGGESTED TIME RANGES	SUGGESTED LEVELS
	—— Daily Focus Skills Transparency 5–3, TCR ✒ 📁	5–10 minutes	L1
	—— Preteaching Vocabulary, TWE, p. 141	5–10 minutes	All levels
	—— Audio Program Chapter 5 🔊	20–25 minutes	All levels

	TEACH MENU		
	Guided Practice		
	—— Activity, TWE, p. 142	5–10 minutes	L2
	—— Cooperative Learning Activity, TWE, p. 142	40–60 minutes	ELL, L1
	—— Meeting Special Needs, TWE, p. 143	25–35 minutes	L1
	—— Interdisciplinary Connections Activity, TWE, p. 144	20–30 minutes	L1
	—— Graphic Organizer Transparencies Strategies and Activities, TCR ✒ 📁	20–25 minutes	All levels
	Independent Practice		
	—— Guided Reading Activity 5–3, TCR 📁	15–20 minutes	ELL, L1

	ASSESS MENU		
	Evaluate		
	—— Section Quiz 5-3, TCR 📁	10–15 minutes	All levels
	—— Interactive Tutor Self-Assessment CD-ROM ⦿	20–30 minutes	All levels
	—— ExamView® Pro Testmaker CD-ROM ⦿	15–20 minutes	All levels
	Reteach		
	—— Reteaching Activity 5–3, TCR 📁	15–20 minutes	ELL, L1
	—— Reading Essentials and Study Guide 5–3, TCR 📁	25–35 minutes	ELL, L1
	Enrich		
	—— Enrichment Activity 5–3, TCR 📁	10–15 minutes	L2, L3
	—— Primary Source Reading 5, TCR 📁	20–30 minutes	All levels

	CLOSE MENU		
	—— Close, TWE, p. 145	10–15 minutes	All levels

See Optional Resources menu on page viii.

Grade _____ Class(es) _____ Date _____ M Tu W Th F

Teacher's Name _____ Date _____

Moving Toward Independence   Section 4 (pp. 147–151)

LOCAL OBJECTIVES	TWE—Teacher Wraparound Edition TCR—Teacher Classroom Resources 📁 Blackline Master ♟ Transparency ⊙ CD-ROM ⊚ DVD ▯ Poster ♫ Music Program ◍ Audio Program ▭ Videocassette ⬤ Internet Resources

	OBJECTIVES
	1. Understand what happened at the Second Continental Congress.
	2. Explore why the Declaration of Independence was drafted.

	FOCUS MENU	SUGGESTED TIME RANGES	SUGGESTED LEVELS
	—— Daily Focus Skills Transparency 5–4, TCR ♟ 📁	15–20 minutes	All levels
	—— Vocabulary PuzzleMaker CD-ROM ⊙	10–15 minutes	All levels
	—— Audio Program Chapter 5 ◍	20–25 minutes	All levels

	TEACH MENU		
	Guided Practice		
	—— Activity, TWE, p. 148	5–10 minutes	L2
	—— Cooperative Learning Activity, TWE, p. 148	40–60 minutes	L2
	—— Meeting Special Needs, TWE, p. 149	10–15 minutes	L1
	—— Interdisciplinary Connections Activity, TWE, p. 150	20–30 minutes	L2
	—— Graphic Organizer Transparencies Strategies and Activities, TCR ♟ 📁	20–25 minutes	All levels
	—— History Online Activity ⬤	15–20 minutes	All levels
	—— Why It Matters Chapter Transparency Strategy and Activity 5, TCR ♟ 📁	25–30 minutes	All levels
	Independent Practice		
	—— Guided Reading Activity 5–4, TCR 📁	15–20 minutes	ELL, L1
	—— Vocabulary Activity 5, TCR 📁	20–30 minutes	All levels
	—— Chapter Skills Activity 5, TCR 📁	20–30 minutes	L1
	—— Critical Thinking Activity 5, TCR 📁	15–20 minutes	L2
	—— Geography and History Activity 5, TCR 📁	10–15 minutes	L1
	—— Time Line Activity 5, TCR 📁	10–15 minutes	L1

	ASSESS MENU		
	Evaluate		
	—— Section Quiz 5–4, TCR 📁	10–15 minutes	All levels
	—— Performance Assessment Activity 5, TCR 📁	25–30 minutes	All levels
	—— Interactive Tutor Self-Assessment CD-ROM ⊙	20–30 minutes	All levels
	—— ExamView® Pro Testmaker CD-ROM ⊙	15–20 minutes	All levels
	Reteach		
	—— Reteaching Activity 5–4, TCR 📁	15–20 minutes	ELL, L1
	—— Reading Essentials and Study Guide 5–4, TCR 📁	25–35 minutes	ELL, L1
	—— Take-Home Review Activity 5, TCR 📁	10–15 minutes	All levels
	—— MindJogger Videoquiz, Chapter 5 ⊚ ▭	20–25 minutes	All levels
	Enrich		
	—— Enrichment Activity 5–4, TCR 📁	10–15 minutes	L2, L3

	CLOSE MENU		
	—— Close, TWE, p. 151	10–15 minutes	All levels

See Optional Resources menu on page viii.

The Early Years

Section 1 *(pp. 162–168)*

LOCAL OBJECTIVES	TWE—Teacher Wraparound Edition TCR—Teacher Classroom Resources 📁 Blackline Master 🔖 Transparency 💿 CD-ROM 💿 DVD 📖 Poster 🎵 Music Program 🎧 Audio Program 📼 Videocassette ➤ Internet Resources

	OBJECTIVES **1.** Understand why some Americans supported the British. **2.** Explain how the Battle of Saratoga marked a turning point in the war.		

	FOCUS MENU	**SUGGESTED TIME RANGES**	**SUGGESTED LEVELS**
	—— Daily Focus Skills Transparency 6–1, TCR 🔖 📁	5–10 minutes	L1
	—— Preteaching Vocabulary, TWE, p. 162	5–10 minutes	All levels
	—— History Online Chapter 6 Overview ➤	15–20 minutes	All levels
	—— Audio Program Chapter 6 🎧	20–25 minutes	All levels

	TEACH MENU **Guided Practice**		
	—— Time Line Activity, TWE, p. 161	5–20 minutes	All levels
	—— Activity, TWE, p. 163	5–10 minutes	L1
	—— Cooperative Learning Activity, TWE, p. 163	40–60 minutes	L2
	—— Meeting Special Needs, TWE, p. 164	20–35 minutes	L1
	—— Interdisciplinary Connections Activity, TWE, p. 165	20–30 minutes	ELL, L3
	—— Critical Thinking Activity, TWE, p. 166	20–25 minutes	L2
	—— Extending the Content, TWE, p. 167	5–10 minutes	All levels
	—— Graphic Organizer Transparencies Strategies and Activities, TCR 🔖 📁	20–25 minutes	All levels
	—— American Art and Architecture 🔖 📁	25–30 minutes	All levels
	—— Why It Matters Chapter Transparency Strategy and Activity 6, TCR 🔖 📁	25–30 minutes	All levels
	Independent Practice		
	—— Guided Reading Activity 6–1, TCR 📁	15–20 minutes	ELL, L1
	—— Reading and Study Skills Foldable, p. 161	10–15 minutes	All levels

	ASSESS MENU **Evaluate**		
	—— Section Quiz 6–1, TCR 📁	10–15 minutes	All levels
	—— Interactive Tutor Self-Assessment CD-ROM 💿	20–30 minutes	All levels
	—— ExamView® Pro Testmaker CD-ROM 💿	15–20 minutes	All levels
	Reteach		
	—— Reteaching Activity 6–1, TCR 📁	15–20 minutes	ELL, L1
	—— Reading Essentials and Study Guide 6–1, TCR 📁	25–35 minutes	ELL, L1
	Enrich		
	—— Enrichment Activity 6–1, TCR 📁	10–15 minutes	L2, L3
	—— Linking Past and Present Activity 6, TCR 📁	15–20 minutes	All levels

	CLOSE MENU		
	—— Close, TWE, p. 168	10–15 minutes	All levels

See Optional Resources menu on page viii.

Grade _____ Class(es) _____ Date _____ M Tu W Th F

Teacher's Name _____ Date _____

The War Continues
Section 2 (pp. 172–176)

LOCAL OBJECTIVES	TWE—Teacher Wraparound Edition TCR—Teacher Classroom Resources		
	📁 Blackline Master 🖌 Transparency 💿 CD-ROM 📀 DVD 📘 Poster		
	🎌 Music Program 🎧 Audio Program 📼 Videocassette 🔗 Internet Resources		

	OBJECTIVES		
	1. Understand why other nations helped the Patriots.		
	2. Describe how Washington's troops survived the winter at Valley Forge.		
	3. Recognize the challenges Americans faced at home as a result of the war.		

	FOCUS MENU	SUGGESTED TIME RANGES	SUGGESTED LEVELS
	—— Daily Focus Skills Transparency 6–2, TCR 🖌 📁	5–10 minutes	L1
	—— Preteaching Vocabulary, TWE, p. 172	5–10 minutes	All levels
	—— Audio Program Chapter 6 🎧	20–25 minutes	All levels

	TEACH MENU		
	Guided Practice		
	—— Activity, TWE, p. 173	5–10 minutes	L1
	—— Cooperative Learning Activity, TWE, p. 173	40–60 minutes	L2
	—— Meeting Special Needs, TWE, p. 174	25–35 minutes	L1
	—— Interdisciplinary Connections Activity, TWE, p. 175	20–30 minutes	ELL, L1
	—— Graphic Organizer Transparencies Strategies and Activities, TCR 🖌 📁	20–25 minutes	All levels
	Independent Practice		
	—— Guided Reading Activity 6–2, TCR 📁	15–20 minutes	ELL, L1

	ASSESS MENU		
	Evaluate		
	—— Section Quiz 6–2, TCR 📁	10–15 minutes	All levels
	—— Interactive Tutor Self-Assessment CD-ROM 💿	20–30 minutes	All levels
	—— ExamView® Pro Testmaker CD-ROM 💿	15–20 minutes	All levels
	Reteach		
	—— Reteaching Activity 6–2, TCR 📁	15–20 minutes	ELL, L1
	—— Reading Essentials and Study Guide 6-2, TCR 📁	25–35 minutes	ELL, L1
	Enrich		
	—— Enrichment Activity 6–2, TCR 📁	10–15 minutes	L2, L3
	—— Primary Source Reading 6, TCR 📁	20–30 minutes	All levels

	CLOSE MENU		
	—— Close, TWE, p. 176	10–15 minutes	All levels

See Optional Resources menu on page viii.

Copyright © by The McGraw-Hill Companies, Inc.

The American Journey

Grade _____ Class(es) _____ Date _____ M Tu W Th F

Teacher's Name _____ Date _____

The War Moves West and South   Section 3 *(pp. 177–182)*

LOCAL OBJECTIVES	TWE—Teacher Wraparound Edition TCR—Teacher Classroom Resources 📁 Blackline Master 🖌 Transparency 💿 CD-ROM 💿 DVD 📖 Poster 🏳 Music Program 🎧 Audio Program 📼 Videocassette 🖱 Internet Resources

	OBJECTIVES
	1. Explain how the war involved Native Americans.
	2. Describe how a new kind of fighting developed in the South.

	FOCUS MENU	**SUGGESTED TIME RANGES**	**SUGGESTED LEVELS**
	—— Daily Focus Skills Transparency 6–3, TCR 🖌 📁	5–10 minutes	L1
	—— Preteaching Vocabulary, TWE, p. 177	5–10 minutes	All levels
	—— Audio Program Chapter 6 🎧	20–25 minutes	All levels
	TEACH MENU		
	Guided Practice		
	—— Activity, TWE, p. 178	5–10 minutes	L2
	—— Cooperative Learning Activity, TWE, p. 178	40–60 minutes	L2
	—— Meeting Special Needs, TWE, p. 179	25–35 minutes	L1
	—— Interdisciplinary Connections Activity, TWE, p. 180	20–30 minutes	ELL, L2
	—— Critical Thinking Activity, TWE, p. 181	20–25 minutes	L1
	—— Graphic Organizer Transparency Strategy and Activity 6, TCR 🖌 📁	15–20 minutes	L2
	Independent Practice		
	—— Guided Reading Activity 6–3, TCR 📁	15–20 minutes	ELL, L1
	ASSESS MENU		
	Evaluate		
	—— Section Quiz 6–3, TCR 📁	10–15 minutes	All levels
	—— Interactive Tutor Self-Assessment CD-ROM 💿	20–30 minutes	All levels
	—— ExamView® Pro Testmaker CD-ROM 💿	15–20 minutes	All levels
	Reteach		
	—— Reteaching Activity 6–3, TCR 📁	15–20 minutes	ELL, L1
	—— Reading Essentials and Study Guide 6–3, TCR 📁	25–35 minutes	ELL, L1
	Enrich		
	—— Enrichment Activity 6–3, TCR 📁	10–15 minutes	L2, L3
	CLOSE MENU		
	—— Close, TWE, p. 182	10–15 minutes	All levels

See Optional Resources menu on page viii.

The War Is Won Section 4 (pp. 183–187)

LOCAL OBJECTIVES	TWE—Teacher Wraparound Edition TCR—Teacher Classroom Resources 📁 Blackline Master ♨ Transparency 💿 CD-ROM ⊙ DVD 📕 Poster 🎵 Music Program 🎧 Audio Program 📼 Videocassette ⌐ Internet Resources

OBJECTIVES
1. Describe how George Washington changed his military strategy.
2. Explain how the Americans won the Revolutionary War despite many disadvantages.

FOCUS MENU	**SUGGESTED TIME RANGES**	**SUGGESTED LEVELS**
—— Daily Focus Skills Transparency 6–4, TCR ♨ 📁	15–20 minutes	All levels
—— Vocabulary PuzzleMaker CD-ROM 💿	10–15 minutes	All levels
—— Audio Program Chapter 6 🎧	20–25 minutes	All levels

TEACH MENU
Guided Practice

—— Activity, TWE, p. 184	5–10 minutes	L1
—— Cooperative Learning Activity, TWE, p. 184	40–60 minutes	L1
—— Meeting Special Needs, TWE, p. 185	10–15 minutes	L1
—— Interdisciplinary Connections Activity, TWE, p. 186	20–30 minutes	ELL, L2
—— Graphic Organizer Transparencies Strategies and Activities, TCR ♨ 📁	20–25 minutes	All levels
—— History Online Activity ⌐	15–20 minutes	All levels

Independent Practice

—— Guided Reading Activity 6–4, TCR 📁	15–20 minutes	ELL, L1
—— Vocabulary Activity 6, TCR 📁	20–30 minutes	All levels
—— Chapter Skills Activity 6, TCR 📁	40–60 minutes	L2
—— Critical Thinking Activity 6, TCR 📁	15–20 minutes	L2
—— Geography and History Activity 6, TCR 📁	15–20 minutes	L1
—— Time Line Activity 6, TCR 📁	10–15 minutes	L1

ASSESS MENU
Evaluate

—— Section Quiz 6–4, TCR 📁	10–15 minutes	All levels
—— Performance Assessment Activity 6, TCR 📁	25–30 minutes	All levels
—— Interactive Tutor Self-Assessment CD-ROM 💿	20–30 minutes	All levels
—— ExamView® Pro Testmaker CD-ROM 💿	15–20 minutes	All levels

Reteach

—— Reteaching Activity 6–4, TCR 📁	15–20 minutes	ELL, L1
—— Reading Essentials and Study Guide 6–4, TCR 📁	25–35 minutes	ELL, L1
—— Take-Home Review Activity 6, TCR 📁	10–15 minutes	All levels
—— MindJogger Videoquiz, Chapter 6 ⊙ 📼	20–25 minutes	All levels

Enrich

—— Enrichment Activity 6–4, TCR 📁	10–15 minutes	L2, L3

CLOSE MENU

—— Close, TWE, p. 187	10–15 minutes	All levels

See Optional Resources menu on page viii.

The Articles of Confederation   Section 1 *(pp. 192–198)*

LOCAL OBJECTIVES	TWE—Teacher Wraparound Edition TCR—Teacher Classroom Resources
	📁 Blackline Master 🖱 Transparency 💿 CD-ROM 💿 DVD 📕 Poster
	🎵 Music Program 🎧 Audio Program 📼 Videocassette ⟿ Internet Resources

	OBJECTIVES		
	1. Examine how the weaknesses of the Articles led to instability.		
	2. Explain how the Confederation Congress dealt with the western lands.		

	FOCUS MENU	**SUGGESTED TIME RANGES**	**SUGGESTED LEVELS**
	____ Daily Focus Skills Transparency 7–1, TCR 🖱 📁	5–10 minutes	L1
	____ Preteaching Vocabulary, TWE, p. 192	5–10 minutes	All levels
	____ History Online Chapter 7 Overview ⟿	15–20 minutes	All levels
	____ Audio Program Chapter 7 🎧	20–25 minutes	All levels
	TEACH MENU		
	Guided Practice		
	____ Time Line Activity, TWE, p. 191	5–10 minutes	All levels
	____ Activity, TWE, p. 193	5–10 minutes	ELL, L1
	____ Cooperative Learning Activity, TWE, p. 193	40–60 minutes	L3
	____ Meeting Special Needs, TWE, p. 194	25–35 minutes	L1
	____ Interdisciplinary Connections Activity, TWE, p. 195	20–30 minutes	L2
	____ Critical Thinking Activity, TWE, p. 196	20–25 minutes	L2
	____ Extending the Content, TWE, p. 197	5–10 minutes	All levels
	____ Graphic Organizer Transparencies Strategies and Activities, TCR 🖱 📁	20–25 minutes	All levels
	____ American Biographies 📁	25–30 minutes	All levels
	Independent Practice		
	____ Guided Reading Activity 7–1, TCR 📁	15–20 minutes	ELL, L1
	____ Reading and Study Skills Foldable, p. 191	10–15 minutes	All levels
	ASSESS MENU		
	Evaluate		
	____ Section Quiz 7–1, TCR 📁	10–15 minutes	All levels
	____ Interactive Tutor Self-Assessment CD-ROM 💿	20–30 minutes	All levels
	____ ExamView® Pro Testmaker CD-ROM 💿	15–20 minutes	All levels
	Reteach		
	____ Reteaching Activity 7–1, TCR 📁	15–20 minutes	ELL, L1
	____ Reading Essentials and Study Guide 7–1, TCR 📁	25–35 minutes	ELL, L1
	Enrich		
	____ Enrichment Activity 7–1, TCR 📁	10–15 minutes	L2, L3
	____ Primary Source Reading 7, TCR 📁	20–30 minutes	All levels
	CLOSE MENU		
	____ Close, TWE, p. 198	10–15 minutes	All levels

See Optional Resources menu on page viii.

Convention and Compromise   Section 2 (pp. 199–205)

LOCAL OBJECTIVES	TWE—Teacher Wraparound Edition TCR—Teacher Classroom Resources 📁 Blackline Master 🖋 Transparency 💿 CD-ROM 💿 DVD 📖 Poster 🎵 Music Program 🎧 Audio Program 📼 Videocassette 🔗 Internet Resources

OBJECTIVES

1. Describe how the Constitutional Convention broke the deadlock over the form the new government would take.

2. Understand how the delegates answered the question of representation.

FOCUS MENU	**SUGGESTED TIME RANGES**	**SUGGESTED LEVELS**
—— Daily Focus Skills Transparency 7–2, TCR 🖋 📁	5–10 minutes	L1
—— Preteaching Vocabulary, TWE, p. 199	5–10 minutes	All levels
—— Audio Program Chapter 7 🎧	20–25 minutes	All levels

TEACH MENU

Guided Practice

—— Activity, TWE, p. 200	5–10 minutes	L1
—— Cooperative Learning Activity, TWE, p. 200	40–60 minutes	L1
—— Meeting Special Needs, TWE, p. 201	25–35 minutes	L1
—— Interdisciplinary Connections Activity, TWE, p. 202	20–30 minutes	L1
—— Critical Thinking Activity, TWE, p. 203	20–25 minutes	L2
—— Extending the Content, TWE, p. 204	5–10 minutes	All levels
—— Graphic Organizer Transparencies Strategies and Activities, TCR 🖋 📁	20–25 minutes	All levels
—— Why It Matters Chapter Transparency Strategy and Activity 7, TCR 🖋 📁	25–30 minutes	All levels

Independent Practice

—— Guided Reading Activity 7–2, TCR 📁	15–20 minutes	ELL, L1

ASSESS MENU

Evaluate

—— Section Quiz 7–2, TCR 📁	10–15 minutes	All levels
—— Interactive Tutor Self-Assessment CD-ROM 💿	20–30 minutes	All levels
—— ExamView® Pro Testmaker CD-ROM 💿	15–20 minutes	All levels
—— History Online Activity 🔗	15–20 minutes	All levels

Reteach

—— Reteaching Activity 7–2, TCR 📁	15–20 minutes	ELL, L1
—— Reading Essentials and Study Guide 7–2, TCR 📁	25–35 minutes	ELL, L1

Enrich

—— Enrichment Activity 7–2, TCR 📁	10–15 minutes	L2, L3
—— Linking Past and Present Activity 7, TCR 📁	15–20 minutes	All levels

CLOSE MENU

—— Close, TWE, p. 205	10–15 minutes	All levels

See Optional Resources menu on page viii.

A New Plan of Government   Section 3 *(pp. 207–213)*

LOCAL OBJECTIVES	TWE—Teacher Wraparound Edition TCR—Teacher Classroom Resources

📁 Blackline Master ✋ Transparency ◉ CD-ROM ◉ DVD 📒 Poster

🎵 Music Program 🎧 Audio Program 📼 Videocassette 🔗 Internet Resources

OBJECTIVES

1. Understand the roots of the Constitution.
2. Explain how the Constitution limits the power of government.

FOCUS MENU	SUGGESTED TIME RANGES	SUGGESTED LEVELS
——— Daily Focus Skills Transparency 7–3, TCR ✋ 📁	5–10 minutes	L1
——— Vocabulary PuzzleMaker CD-ROM ◉	5–10 minutes	All levels
——— Audio Program Chapter 7 🎧	20–25 minutes	All levels

TEACH MENU

Guided Practice

——— Activity, TWE, p. 208	5–10 minutes	L2
——— Cooperative Learning Activity, TWE, p. 208	40–60 minutes	ELL, L1
——— Meeting Special Needs, TWE, p. 209	25–35 minutes	L1
——— Interdisciplinary Connections Activity, TWE, p. 210	20–30 minutes	L2
——— Critical Thinking Activity, TWE, p. 211	20–25 minutes	L2
——— Graphic Organizer Transparency Strategy and Activity 7, TCR ✋ 📁	15–20 minutes	L2

Independent Practice

——— Guided Reading Activity 7–3, TCR 📁	15–20 minutes	ELL, L1
——— Vocabulary Activity 7, TCR 📁	20–30 minutes	All levels
——— Chapter Skills Activity 7, TCR 📁	40–60 minutes	L2, L3
——— Critical Thinking Activity 7, TCR 📁	20–30 minutes	L2, L3
——— Geography and History Activity 7, TCR 📁	15–20 minutes	L1
——— Time Line Activity 7, TCR 📁	30–40 minutes	L1

ASSESS MENU

Evaluate

——— Section Quiz 7–3, TCR 📁	10–15 minutes	All levels
——— Performance Assessment Activity 7, TCR 📁	25–30 minutes	All levels
——— Interactive Tutor Self-Assessment CD-ROM ◉	20–30 minutes	All levels
——— ExamView® Pro Testmaker CD-ROM ◉	15–20 minutes	All levels

Reteach

——— Reteaching Activity 7–3, TCR 📁	15–20 minutes	ELL, L1
——— Reading Essentials and Study Guide 7–3, TCR 📁	25–35 minutes	ELL, L1
——— Take-Home Review Activity 7, TCR 📁	10–15 minutes	All levels
——— MindJogger Videoquiz, Chapter 7 ◉ 📼	20–25 minutes	All levels

Enrich

——— Enrichment Activity 7–3, TCR 📁	10–15 minutes	L2, L3

CLOSE MENU

——— Close, TWE, p. 213	10–15 minutes	All levels

See Optional Resources menu on page viii.

Grade _____ Class(es) _____ Date _____ M Tu W Th F

Teacher's Name _____ Date _____

REPRODUCIBLE LESSON PLAN: **Civics in Action: A Citizenship Handbook**

The Constitution
Section 1 *(pp. 217–222)*

LOCAL OBJECTIVES	TWE—Teacher Wraparound Edition TCR—Teacher Classroom Resources 📁 Blackline Master 🔖 Transparency 💿 CD-ROM ⊙ DVD 🖼 Poster 🎵 Music Program 🎧 Audio Program 📼 Videocassette 💾 Internet Resources

OBJECTIVES
1. Explain why the Constitution is the nation's most important document.
2. Identify the goals of the Constitution.
3. Describe the principles that form the basis of the Constitution.

FOCUS MENU	SUGGESTED TIME RANGES	SUGGESTED LEVEL
—— Beginning the Handbook, TWE, p. 216	5–10 minutes	L1
—— Bellringer Motivational Activity, TWE, p. 217	10–15 minutes	All levels
—— Guide to Reading, TWE, p. 217	15–20 minutes	All levels
—— Vocabulary PuzzleMaker CD-ROM 💿	15–20 minutes	All levels

TEACH MENU
Guided Practice

—— Activity, TWE, p. 218	5–10 minutes	ELL, L1
—— Cooperative Learning Activity, TWE, p. 218	40–60 minutes	L2
—— Meeting Special Needs, TWE, p. 219	25–35 minutes	L1
—— Interdisciplinary Connections Activity, TWE, p. 220	20–30 minutes	L1
—— Critical Thinking Activity, TWE, p. 221	20–25 minutes	L2
—— Civics in Action: Activities, Quizzes, and Tests, Transparency 1 🔖 📁	20–25 minutes	L2

Independent Practice

—— Civics in Action: Activities, Quizzes, and Tests, Guided Reading Activity 1 📁	15–20 minutes	ELL, L1
—— The Living Constitution, TCR 📁	Time will vary	All levels

ASSESS MENU
Evaluate

—— Civics in Action: Activities, Quizzes, and Tests, Constitution Pretest 📁	25–35 minutes	L1
—— Civics in Action: Activities, Quizzes, and Tests, Section Quiz 1 📁	10–15 minutes	All levels

Enrich

—— Civics in Action: Activities, Quizzes, and Tests, Enrichment Activity 1 📁	15–20 minutes	L2
—— Supreme Court Cases Studies	20–30 minutes	L2

CLOSE MENU

—— Close, TWE, p. 222	10–15 minutes	All levels

See Optional Resources menu on page viii.

The American Journey

Grade _____ Class(es) _____ Date _____ M Tu W Th F

Teacher's Name _____ Date _____

The Federal Government Section 2 *(pp. 223–227)*

LOCAL OBJECTIVES	TWE—Teacher Wraparound Edition TCR—Teacher Classroom Resources 📁 Blackline Master 🖎 Transparency ◉ CD-ROM ◉ DVD 📙 Poster 🎵 Music Program 🔊 Audio Program 📺 Videocassette ✒ Internet Resources		
	OBJECTIVES **1.** Explain the goals of the three branches of government. **2.** Identify the powers of the three branches of government.		
	FOCUS MENU	**SUGGESTED TIME RANGES**	**SUGGESTED LEVEL**
	—— Bellringer Motivational Activity, TWE, p. 223	10–15 minutes	All levels
	—— Preteaching Vocabulary, TWE, p. 223	15–20 minutes	All levels
	—— Vocabulary PuzzleMaker CD-ROM ◉	15–20 minutes	All levels
	TEACH MENU **Guided Practice**		
	—— Activity, TWE, p. 224	5–10 minutes	ELL, L1
	—— Cooperative Learning Activity, TWE, p. 224	20–30 minutes	L1
	—— Meeting Special Needs, TWE, p. 225	25–35 minutes	L1
	—— Interdisciplinary Connections Activity, TWE, p. 226	20–30 minutes	L2
	—— Civics in Action: Activities, Quizzes, and Tests, Transparencies 2 and 3 🖎 📁	20–30 minutes	L2
	Independent Practice		
	—— Civics in Action: Activities, Quizzes, and Tests, Guided Reading Activity 2 📁	15–20 minutes	ELL, L1
	—— The Living Constitution, TCR 📁	Time will vary	All levels
	ASSESS MENU **Evaluate**		
	—— Civics in Action: Activities, Quizzes, and Tests, Section Quiz 2 📁	10–15 minutes	All levels
	Enrich		
	—— Civics in Action: Activities, Quizzes, and Tests, Enrichment Activity 2 📁	15–20 minutes	L2
	CLOSE MENU —— Close, TWE, p. 227	10–15 minutes	All levels

See Optional Resources menu on page viii.

Citizens' Rights and Responsibilities Section 3 (pp. 228–230)

LOCAL OBJECTIVES	TWE—Teacher Wraparound Edition TCR—Teacher Classroom Resources
	📁 Blackline Master 🖋 Transparency 💿 CD-ROM 💿 DVD 📕 Poster
	🎵 Music Program 🎧 Audio Program 📼 Videocassette 🔗 Internet Resources

	OBJECTIVES
	1. Identify where the rights of U.S. citizens come from.
	2. Explain the rights and responsibilities of U.S. citizens.

	FOCUS MENU	**SUGGESTED TIME RANGES**	**SUGGESTED LEVEL**
	____ Bellringer Motivational Activity, TWE, p. 228	10–15 minutes	All levels
	____ Preteaching Vocabulary, TWE, p. 228	15–20 minutes	All levels
	____ Vocabulary PuzzleMaker CD-ROM 💿	15–20 minutes	All levels

	TEACH MENU		
	Guided Practice		
	____ Activity, TWE, p. 229	5-10 minutes	L1
	____ Cooperative Learning Activity, TWE, p. 229	40–60 minutes	L1
	____ Civics in Action: Activities, Quizzes, and Tests, Transparency 4 🖋 📁	20–25 minutes	L2
	Independent Practice		
	____ Civics in Action: Activities, Quizzes, and Tests, Guided Reading Activity 3 📁	15–20 minutes	ELL, L1
	____ The Living Constitution, TCR 📁	Time will vary	All levels

	ASSESS MENU		
	Evaluate		
	____ Civics in Action: Activities, Quizzes, and Tests, Section Quiz 3 📁	10–15 minutes	All levels
	____ Civics in Action: Activities, Quizzes, and Tests, Constitution Posttest	25–35 minutes	All levels
	Enrich		
	____ Civics in Action: Activities, Quizzes, and Tests, Enrichment Activity 3 📁	15–20 minutes	L2

	CLOSE MENU		
	____ Close, TWE, p. 230	10-15 minutes	All levels

See Optional Resources menu on page viii.

Grade _____   Class(es) _____   Date _____   M Tu W Th F

Teacher's Name _____   Date _____

The Constitution of the United States   *(pp. 232–253)*

LOCAL OBJECTIVES	TWE—Teacher Wraparound Edition TCR—Teacher Classroom Resources
	📁 Blackline Master 🔦 Transparency 💿 CD-ROM 📀 DVD 📱 Poster
	🎵 Music Program 🎧 Audio Program 📼 Videocassette 🖱️ Internet Resources

OBJECTIVES

1. Describe the purpose of the United States Constitution.
2. Identify the branches of government and their powers.
3. Analyze the amendments to the United States Constitution.

FOCUS MENU	SUGGESTED TIME RANGES	SUGGESTED LEVEL
—— Bellringer Motivational Activity, TWE, pp. 232, 238, 240, 242, 244	10–15 minutes	All levels

TEACH MENU
Guided Practice

	SUGGESTED TIME RANGES	SUGGESTED LEVEL
—— Activity, TWE, pp. 233–237, 239, 241–243, 245–251	35–40 minutes	L1, L2, L3
—— Meeting Special Needs, TWE, p. 232	5–10 minutes	L1
—— Extending the Content, TWE, pp. 233, 237, 238, 240, 243, 244, 246, 247, 248, 252	5–10 minutes	All levels
—— Critical Thinking Activity, TWE, pp. 234, 251	20–25 minutes	L2
—— Critical Thinking Activity, TWE, pp. 236, 249	15–20 minutes	L1
—— Critical Thinking Activity, TWE, pp. 239, 241, 245	20–25 minutes	L3
—— Cooperative Learning Activity, TWE, p. 235	40–60 minutes	L1
—— Cooperative Learning Activity, TWE, p. 242	40–60 minutes	L3
—— Cooperative Learning Activity, TWE, p. 250	25–30 minutes	L1
—— Cooperative Learning Activity, TWE, p. 253	30–40 minutes	L1

Independent Practice

—— The Living Constitution, TCR 📁	Time will vary	Various levels

See Optional Resources menu on page viii.

The First President

Section 1 (*pp. 258–262*)

LOCAL OBJECTIVES	TWE—Teacher Wraparound Edition · Blackline Master · Transparency · Music Program · Audio Program	TCR—Teacher Classroom Resources · CD-ROM · DVD · Poster · Videocassette · Internet Resources		
	OBJECTIVES **1.** Describe what actions were taken to launch the new government. **2.** Explain how Hamilton proposed to strengthen the economy.			
	FOCUS MENU		**SUGGESTED TIME RANGES**	**SUGGESTED LEVELS**
	—— Daily Focus Skills Transparency 8–1, TCR		5–10 minutes	L1
	—— Preteaching Vocabulary, TWE, p. 258		5–10 minutes	All levels
	—— History Online Chapter 8 Overview		15–20 minutes	All levels
	—— Audio Program Chapter 8		20–25 minutes	All levels
	TEACH MENU **Guided Practice**			
	—— Time Line Activity, TWE, p. 257		10–15 minutes	L1
	—— Activity, TWE, p. 259		5–10 minutes	L1
	—— Cooperative Learning Activity, TWE, p. 259		40–60 minutes	ELL, L1
	—— Meeting Special Needs, TWE, p. 260		25–35 minutes	L1
	—— Interdisciplinary Connections Activity, TWE, p. 261		20–30 minutes	L2
	—— Graphic Organizer Transparency Strategy and Activity 8, TCR		15–20 minutes	L2
	Independent Practice			
	—— Guided Reading Activity 8–1, TCR		15–20 minutes	ELL, L1
	—— Reading and Study Skills Foldable, p. 257		10–15 minutes	All levels
	ASSESS MENU **Evaluate**			
	—— Section Quiz 8–1, TCR		10–15 minutes	All levels
	—— Interactive Tutor Self-Assessment CD-ROM		20–30 minutes	All levels
	—— ExamView® Pro Testmaker CD-ROM		15–20 minutes	All levels
	Reteach			
	—— Reteaching Activity 8–1, TCR		15–20 minutes	ELL, L1
	—— Reading Essentials and Study Guide 8–1, TCR		25–35 minutes	ELL, L1
	Enrich			
	—— Enrichment Activity 8–1, TCR		10–15 minutes	L2, L3
	—— Primary Source Reading 8, TCR		20–30 minutes	All levels
	CLOSE MENU			
	—— Close, TWE, p. 262		10–15 minutes	All levels

See Optional Resources menu on page viii.

Early Challenges

Section 2 (pp. 263–266)

LOCAL OBJECTIVES	TWE—Teacher Wraparound Edition TCR—Teacher Classroom Resources
	🗂 Blackline Master 🔥 Transparency 🔘 CD-ROM 🔘 DVD 📗 Poster
	🏴 Music Program 🔊 Audio Program 📺 Videocassette ⌇ Internet Resources

OBJECTIVES

1. Understand how the federal government asserted its power in the West.

2. Examine how the United States tried to stay out of European conflicts.

FOCUS MENU	SUGGESTED TIME RANGES	SUGGESTED LEVELS
—— Daily Focus Skills Transparency 8–2, TCR 🔥 🗂	5–10 minutes	L1
—— Preteaching Vocabulary, TWE, p. 263	5–10 minutes	All levels
—— Audio Program Chapter 8 🔊	20–25 minutes	All levels

TEACH MENU

Guided Practice

—— Activity, TWE, p. 264	5–10 minutes	L1
—— Cooperative Learning Activity, TWE, p. 264	40–60 minutes	ELL, L1
—— Meeting Special Needs, TWE, p. 265	25–35 minutes	L1
—— Graphic Organizer Transparencies Strategies and Activities, TCR 🔥 🗂	20–25 minutes	All levels

Independent Practice

—— Guided Reading Activity 8–2, TCR 🗂	15–20 minutes	ELL, L1

ASSESS MENU

Evaluate

—— Section Quiz 8–2, TCR 🗂	10–15 minutes	All levels
—— Interactive Tutor Self-Assessment CD-ROM 🔘	20–30 minutes	All levels
—— ExamView® Pro Testmaker CD-ROM 🔘	15–20 minutes	All levels

Reteach

—— Reteaching Activity 8–2, TCR 🗂	15–20 minutes	ELL, L1
—— Reading Essentials and Study Guide 8–2, TCR 🗂	25–35 minutes	ELL, L1

Enrich

—— Enrichment Activity 8–2, TCR 🗂	10–15 minutes	L2, L3
—— Linking Past and Present Activity 8, TCR 🗂	15–20 minutes	All levels

CLOSE MENU

—— Close, TWE, p. 266	10–15 minutes	All levels

See Optional Resources menu on page viii.

The First Political Parties
Section 3 (pp. 267–272)

LOCAL OBJECTIVES	TWE—Teacher Wraparound Edition TCR—Teacher Classroom Resources 📁 Blackline Master ♟ Transparency 💿 CD-ROM ⊙ DVD 📕 Poster 🎵 Music Program 🎧 Audio Program 📼 Videocassette 🖱 Internet Resources		

OBJECTIVES

1. Describe how political parties got started and what positions they supported.
2. Explain how John Adams and Thomas Jefferson became candidates of opposing parties in the election of 1796.

FOCUS MENU	SUGGESTED TIME RANGES	SUGGESTED LEVELS
____ Daily Focus Skills Transparency 8–3, TCR ♟ 📁	5–10 minutes	L1
____ Vocabulary PuzzleMaker CD-ROM 💿	5–10 minutes	All levels
____ Audio Program Chapter 8 🎧	20–25 minutes	All levels

TEACH MENU

Guided Practice

____ Activity, TWE, p. 268	5–10 minutes	L1
____ Cooperative Learning Activity, TWE, p. 268	40–60 minutes	L2
____ Meeting Special Needs, TWE, p. 269	25–35 minutes	L1
____ Interdisciplinary Connections Activity, TWE, p. 270	20–30 minutes	L2
____ Critical Thinking Activity, TWE, p. 271	20–25 minutes	L3
____ Graphic Organizer Transparencies Strategies and Activities, TCR ♟ 📁	20–25 minutes	All levels

Independent Practice

____ Guided Reading Activity 8–3, TCR 📁	15–20 minutes	ELL, L1
____ Vocabulary Activity 8, TCR 📁	20–30 minutes	All levels
____ Chapter Skills Activity 8, TCR 📁	10–15 minutes	L1
____ Critical Thinking Activity 8, TCR 📁	15–20 minutes	L2
____ Geography and History Activity 8, TCR 📁	20–30 minutes	L1
____ Time Line Activity 8, TCR 📁	10–15 minutes	All levels

ASSESS MENU

Evaluate

____ Section Quiz 8–3, TCR 📁	10–15 minutes	All levels
____ Performance Assessment Activity 8, TCR 📁	25–30 minutes	All levels
____ Interactive Tutor Self-Assessment CD-ROM 💿	20–30 minutes	All levels
____ ExamView® Pro Testmaker CD-ROM 💿	15–20 minutes	All levels
____ History Online Activity 🖱	15–20 minutes	All levels

Reteach

____ Reteaching Activity 8–3, TCR 📁	15–20 minutes	ELL, L1
____ Reading Essentials and Study Guide 8–3, TCR 📁	25–35 minutes	ELL, L1
____ Take-Home Review Activity 8, TCR 📁	10–15 minutes	All levels
____ MindJogger Videoquiz, Chapter 8 ⊙ 📼	20–25 minutes	All levels

Enrich

____ Enrichment Activity 8–3, TCR 📁	10–15 minutes	L2, L3

CLOSE MENU

____ Close, TWE, p. 272	10–15 minutes	All levels

See Optional Resources menu on page viii.

The Republicans Take Power   Section 1 *(pp. 278–281)*

LOCAL OBJECTIVES	TWE—Teacher Wraparound Edition TCR—Teacher Classroom Resources

Blackline Master   Transparency   CD-ROM   DVD   Poster
Music Program   Audio Program   Videocassette   Internet Resources

OBJECTIVES

1. Discuss how the election of 1800 was resolved.

2. Explain how the Supreme Court was strengthened.

FOCUS MENU	SUGGESTED TIME RANGES	SUGGESTED LEVELS
____ Daily Focus Skills Transparency 9–1, TCR	5–10 minutes	L1
____ Preteaching Vocabulary, TWE, p. 278	5–10 minutes	All levels
____ History Online Chapter 9 Overview	15–20 minutes	All levels
____ Audio Program Chapter 9	20–25 minutes	All levels

TEACH MENU

Guided Practice

____ Time Line Activity, TWE, p. 277	5–10 minutes	All levels
____ Activity, TWE, p. 279	15–20 minutes	L1
____ Cooperative Learning Activity, TWE, p. 279	40–60 minutes	ELL, L1
____ Meeting Special Needs, TWE, p. 280	25–35 minutes	L1
____ Graphic Organizer Transparency Strategy and Activity 9, TCR	15–20 minutes	L2
____ American Art and Architecture	25–30 minutes	All levels
____ Why It Matters Chapter Transparency Strategy and Activity 9, TCR	25–30 minutes	All levels

Independent Practice

____ Guided Reading Activity 9–1, TCR	15–20 minutes	ELL, L1
____ Reading and Study Skills Foldable, p. 277	10–15 minutes	All levels

ASSESS MENU

Evaluate

____ Section Quiz 9–1, TCR	10–15 minutes	All levels
____ Interactive Tutor Self-Assessment CD-ROM	20–30 minutes	All levels
____ ExamView® Pro Testmaker CD-ROM	15–20 minutes	All levels
____ History Online Activity	15–20 minutes	All levels

Reteach

____ Reteaching Activity 9–1, TCR	15–20 minutes	ELL, L1
____ Reading Essentials and Study Guide 9–1, TCR	25–35 minutes	ELL, L1

Enrich

____ Enrichment Activity 9–1, TCR	10–15 minutes	L2, L3

CLOSE MENU

____ Close, TWE, p. 281	10–15 minutes	All levels

See Optional Resources menu on page viii.

The Louisiana Purchase

Section 2 *(pp. 282–285)*

LOCAL OBJECTIVES	TWE—Teacher Wraparound Edition · · · · · · · · · · TCR—Teacher Classroom Resources Blackline Master Transparency CD-ROM DVD Poster Music Program Audio Program Videocassette Internet Resources		
	OBJECTIVES **1.** Discuss how the United States expanded in the early 1800s. **2.** Review the expeditions of explorers such as Lewis and Clark.		
	FOCUS MENU	**SUGGESTED TIME RANGES**	**SUGGESTED LEVELS**
	—— Daily Focus Skills Transparency 9–2, TCR	5–10 minutes	L1
	—— Preteaching Vocabulary, TWE, p. 282	5–10 minutes	All levels
	—— Audio Program Chapter 9	20–25 minutes	All levels
	TEACH MENU **Guided Practice**		
	—— Activity, TWE, p. 283	5–10 minutes	L1
	—— Cooperative Learning Activity, TWE, p. 283	40–60 minutes	ELL, L1
	—— Meeting Special Needs, TWE, p. 284	25–35 minutes	L1
	—— Graphic Organizer Transparencies Strategies and Activities, TCR	20–25 minutes	All levels
	Independent Practice		
	—— Guided Reading Activity 9–2, TCR	15–20 minutes	ELL, L1
	ASSESS MENU **Evaluate**		
	—— Section Quiz 9–2, TCR	10–15 minutes	All levels
	—— Interactive Tutor Self-Assessment CD-ROM	20–30 minutes	All levels
	—— ExamView® Pro Testmaker CD-ROM	15–20 minutes	All levels
	Reteach		
	—— Reteaching Activity 9–2, TCR	15–20 minutes	ELL, L1
	—— Reading Essentials and Study Guide 9–2, TCR	25–35 minutes	ELL, L1
	Enrich		
	—— Enrichment Activity 9–2, TCR	10–15 minutes	L2, L3
	—— Linking Past and Present Activity 9, TCR	15–20 minutes	All levels
	CLOSE MENU		
	—— Close, TWE, p. 285	10–15 minutes	All levels

See Optional Resources menu on page viii.

A Time of Conflict
Section 3 *(pp. 288–294)*

LOCAL OBJECTIVES	TWE—Teacher Wraparound Edition TCR—Teacher Classroom Resources
	🗂 Blackline Master 🔦 Transparency 💿 CD-ROM 💿 DVD 📕 Poster
	🎵 Music Program 🎧 Audio Program 📼 Videocassette ⬤⟋ Internet Resources

		SUGGESTED TIME RANGES	SUGGESTED LEVELS
	OBJECTIVES		
	1. Explain why Tecumseh built a Native American confederacy.		
	2. Discuss why the War Hawks wanted to go to war.		
	FOCUS MENU		
	____ Daily Focus Skills Transparency 9–3, TCR 🔦 🗂	5–10 minutes	L1
	____ Preteaching Vocabulary, TWE, p. 288	5–10 minutes	All levels
	____ Audio Program Chapter 9 🎧	20–25 minutes	All levels
	TEACH MENU		
	Guided Practice		
	____ Activity, TWE, p. 289	5–10 minutes	L1
	____ Cooperative Learning Activity, TWE, p. 289	40–60 minutes	L2
	____ Meeting Special Needs, TWE, p. 290	25–35 minutes	L1
	____ Interdisciplinary Connections Activity, TWE, p. 291	20–30 minutes	L2
	____ Critical Thinking Activity, TWE, p. 292	20–25 minutes	L3
	____ Extending the Content, TWE, p. 293	5–10 minutes	All levels
	____ Graphic Organizer Transparencies Strategies and Activities, TCR 🔦 🗂	20–25 minutes	All levels
	Independent Practice		
	____ Guided Reading Activity 9–3, TCR 🗂	15–20 minutes	ELL, L1
	ASSESS MENU		
	Evaluate		
	____ Section Quiz 9–3, TCR 🗂	10–15 minutes	All levels
	____ Interactive Tutor Self-Assessment CD-ROM 💿	20–30 minutes	All levels
	____ ExamView® Pro Testmaker CD-ROM 💿	15–20 minutes	All levels
	Reteach		
	____ Reteaching Activity 9–3, TCR 🗂	15–20 minutes	ELL, L1
	____ Reading Essentials and Study Guide 9–3, TCR 🗂	25–35 minutes	ELL, L1
	Enrich		
	____ Enrichment Activity 9–3, TCR 🗂	10–15 minutes	L2, L3
	____ Primary Source Reading 9, TCR 🗂	20–30 minutes	All levels
	CLOSE MENU		
	____ Close, TWE, p. 294	10–15 minutes	All levels

See Optional Resources menu on page viii.

Grade _____ Class(es) _____ Date _____ M Tu W Th F

Teacher's Name _____ Date _____

The War of 1812   Section 4 *(pp. 296–300)*

LOCAL OBJECTIVES	TWE—Teacher Wraparound Edition TCR—Teacher Classroom Resources 📁 Blackline Master ⚑ Transparency 💿 CD-ROM 💿 DVD 📖 Poster 🎵 Music Program 🎧 Audio Program 📼 Videocassette 🔗 Internet Resources

	OBJECTIVES
	1. Describe how the British seized and set fire to Washington, D.C.
	2. Explain why Andrew Jackson fought a battle after the war was over.

	FOCUS MENU	**SUGGESTED TIME RANGES**	**SUGGESTED LEVELS**
	____ Daily Focus Skills Transparency 9–4, TCR ⚑ 📁	5–10 minutes	L1
	____ Vocabulary PuzzleMaker CD-ROM 💿	5–10 minutes	All levels
	____ Audio Program Chapter 9 🎧	20–25 minutes	All levels

	TEACH MENU		
	Guided Practice		
	____ Activity, TWE, p. 297	5–10 minutes	L3
	____ Cooperative Learning Activity, TWE, p. 297	40–60 minutes	L1
	____ Meeting Special Needs, TWE, p. 298	25–35 minutes	L1
	____ Interdisciplinary Connections Activity, TWE, p. 299	20–30 minutes	L2
	____ Graphic Organizer Transparencies Strategies and Activities, TCR ⚑ 📁	20–25 minutes	All levels
	Independent Practice		
	____ Guided Reading Activity 9–4, TCR 📁	15–20 minutes	ELL, L1
	____ Vocabulary Activity 9, TCR 📁	20–30 minutes	All levels
	____ Chapter Skills Activity 9, TCR 📁	20–30 minutes	All levels
	____ Critical Thinking Activity 9, TCR 📁	15–20 minutes	L2
	____ Geography and History Activity 9, TCR 📁	20–30 minutes	L1
	____ Time Line Activity 9, TCR 📁	10–15 minutes	All levels

	ASSESS MENU		
	Evaluate		
	____ Section Quiz 9–4, TCR 📁	10–15 minutes	All levels
	____ Performance Assessment Activity 9, TCR 📁	25–30 minutes	All levels
	____ Interactive Tutor Self-Assessment CD-ROM 💿	20–30 minutes	All levels
	____ ExamView® Pro Testmaker CD-ROM 💿	15–20 minutes	All levels
	Reteach		
	____ Reteaching Activity 9–4, TCR 📁	15–20 minutes	ELL, L1
	____ Reading Essentials and Study Guide 9–4, TCR 📁	25–35 minutes	ELL, L1
	____ Take-Home Review Activity 9, TCR 📁	10–15 minutes	All levels
	____ MindJogger Videoquiz, Chapter 9 💿 📼	20–25 minutes	All levels
	Enrich		
	____ Enrichment Activity 9–4, TCR 📁	10–15 minutes	L2, L3

	CLOSE MENU		
	____ Close, TWE, p. 300	10–15 minutes	All levels

See Optional Resources menu on page viii.

Economic Growth

Section 1 *(pp. 306–311)*

LOCAL OBJECTIVES	TWE—Teacher Wraparound Edition 🗀 Blackline Master 🔖 Transparency ⚑ Music Program 🎧 Audio Program	TCR—Teacher Classroom Resources ⊙ CD-ROM ⊙ DVD 📕 Poster 📼 Videocassette ➿ Internet Resources		
	OBJECTIVES **1.** Describe how the Industrial Revolution began in the United States. **2.** Describe how the United States changed as it became more economically independent.			
	FOCUS MENU		**SUGGESTED TIME RANGES**	**SUGGESTED LEVEL**
	____ Daily Focus Skills Transparency 10–1, TCR 🔖 🗀		5–10 minutes	L1
	____ Preteaching Vocabulary, TWE, p. 306		5–10 minutes	All levels
	____ History Online Chapter 10 Overview ➿		15–20 minutes	All levels
	____ Audio Program Chapter 10 🎧		20–25 minutes	All levels
	TEACH MENU **Guided Practice**			
	____ Time Line Activity, TWE, p. 305		5–10 minutes	All levels
	____ Activity, TWE, p. 307		5–10 minutes	ELL, L1
	____ Cooperative Learning Activity, TWE, p. 307		40–60 minutes	ELL, L2
	____ Meeting Special Needs, TWE, p. 308		25–35 minutes	L1
	____ Interdisciplinary Connections Activity, TWE, p. 309		20–30 minutes	L2
	____ Critical Thinking Activity, TWE, p. 310		20–25 minutes	L2
	____ Graphic Organizer Transparencies Strategies and Activities, TCR 🔖 🗀		20–25 minutes	All levels
	____ Why It Matters Chapter Transparency Strategy and Activity 10, TCR 🔖 🗀		25–30 minutes	All levels
	Independent Practice			
	____ Guided Reading Activity 10–1, TCR 🗀		15–20 minutes	ELL, L1
	____ Reading and Study Skills Foldable, p. 305		10–15 minutes	All levels
	ASSESS MENU **Evaluate**			
	____ Section Quiz 10–1, TCR 🗀		10–15 minutes	All levels
	____ Interactive Tutor Self-Assessment CD-ROM ⊙		20–30 minutes	All levels
	____ ExamView® Pro Testmaker CD-ROM ⊙		15–20 minutes	All levels
	Reteach			
	____ Reteaching Activity 10–1, TCR 🗀		15–20 minutes	ELL, L1
	____ Reading Essentials and Study Guide 10–1, TCR 🗀		25–35 minutes	ELL, L1
	Enrich			
	____ Enrichment Activity 10–1, TCR 🗀		10–15 minutes	L2, L3
	____ Primary Source Reading 10, TCR 🗀		20–30 minutes	All levels
	CLOSE MENU			
	____ Close, TWE, p. 311		10–15 minutes	All levels

See Optional Resources menu on page viii.

The American Journey

Grade _____ Class(es) _____ Date _____ M Tu W Th F

Teacher's Name _____ Date _____

Westward Bound

Section 2 *(pp. 314–319)*

LOCAL OBJECTIVES	TWE—Teacher Wraparound Edition TCR—Teacher Classroom Resources 🗀 Blackline Master ✍ Transparency 💿 CD-ROM 💿 DVD 📕 Poster 🎵 Music Program 🔊 Audio Program 📼 Videocassette ➷ Internet Resources		
	OBJECTIVES **1.** Explain how transportation improved in the early 1800s. **2.** Understand how Western settlements affected the nation's economy and politics.		
	FOCUS MENU	**SUGGESTED TIME RANGES**	**SUGGESTED LEVEL**
	—— Daily Focus Skills Transparency 10–2, TCR ✍ 🗀	5–10 minutes	L1
	—— Preteaching Vocabulary, TWE, p. 314	5–10 minutes	All levels
	—— Audio Program Chapter 10 🔊	20–25 minutes	All levels
	TEACH MENU **Guided Practice**		
	—— Activity, TWE, p. 315	5–10 minutes	ELL, L1
	—— Cooperative Learning Activity, TWE, p. 315	40–60 minutes	L2
	—— Meeting Special Needs, TWE, p. 316	25–35 minutes	L1
	—— Interdisciplinary Connections Activity, TWE, p. 317	20–30 minutes	ELL, L2
	—— Critical Thinking Activity, TWE, p. 318	20–25 minutes	L2
	—— Graphic Organizer Transparency Strategy and Activity 10, TCR ✍ 🗀	15–20 minutes	L2
	Independent Practice		
	—— Guided Reading Activity 10–2, TCR 🗀	15–20 minutes	ELL, L1
	ASSESS MENU **Evaluate**		
	—— Section Quiz 10–2, TCR 🗀	10–15 minutes	All levels
	—— Interactive Tutor Self-Assessment CD-ROM 💿	20–30 minutes	All levels
	—— ExamView® Pro Testmaker CD-ROM 💿	15–20 minutes	All levels
	Reteach		
	—— Reteaching Activity 10–2, TCR 🗀	15–20 minutes	ELL, L1
	—— Reading Essentials and Study Guide 10–2, TCR 🗀	25–35 minutes	ELL, L1
	Enrich		
	—— Enrichment Activity 10–2, TCR 🗀	10–15 minutes	L2, L3
	—— Linking Past and Present Activity 10, TCR 🗀	15–20 minutes	All levels
	CLOSE MENU		
	—— Close, TWE, p. 319	10–15 minutes	All levels

See Optional Resources menu on page viii.

Grade _____ Class(es) _____ Date _____ M Tu W Th F

Teacher's Name _____ Date _____

REPRODUCIBLE LESSON PLAN 10–3

Unity and Sectionalism   Section 3 *(pp. 321–327)*

LOCAL OBJECTIVES	TWE—Teacher Wraparound Edition TCR—Teacher Classroom Resources 📁 Blackline Master 🖐 Transparency 💿 CD-ROM 💿 DVD 📘 Poster 🎵 Music Program 🎧 Audio Program 📼 Videocassette 🔌 Internet Resources		
	OBJECTIVES **1.** Describe why sectional differences grew in the 1820s. **2.** Identify the effect the Monroe Doctrine had on foreign policy.		
	FOCUS MENU	**SUGGESTED TIME RANGES**	**SUGGESTED LEVEL**
	—— Daily Focus Skills Transparency 10–3, TCR 🖐 📁	5–10 minutes	L1
	—— Vocabulary PuzzleMaker CD-ROM 💿	5–10 minutes	All levels
	—— Audio Program Chapter 10 🎧	20–25 minutes	All levels
	TEACH MENU **Guided Practice**		
	—— Activity, TWE, p. 322	5–10 minutes	L1
	—— Cooperative Learning Activity, TWE, p. 322	40–60 minutes	ELL, L1
	—— Meeting Special Needs, TWE, p. 323	25–35 minutes	L1
	—— Interdisciplinary Connections Activity, TWE, p. 324	20–30 minutes	L2
	—— Critical Thinking Activity, TWE, p. 325	20–25 minutes	L2
	—— Extending the Content, TWE, p. 326	5–10 minutes	All levels
	—— Graphic Organizer Transparencies Strategies and Activities, TCR 🖐 📁	20–25 minutes	All levels
	Independent Practice		
	—— Guided Reading Activity 10–3, TCR 📁	15–20 minutes	ELL, L1
	—— Vocabulary Activity 10, TCR 📁	20–30 minutes	All levels
	—— Chapter Skills Activity 10, TCR 📁	15–20 minutes	All levels
	—— Critical Thinking Activity 10, TCR 📁	15–20 minutes	L1
	—— Geography and History Activity 10, TCR 📁	15–20 minutes	L1
	—— Time Line Activity 10, TCR 📁	10–15 minutes	All levels
	ASSESS MENU **Evaluate**		
	—— Section Quiz 10–3, TCR 📁	10–15 minutes	All levels
	—— Performance Assessment Activity 10, TCR 📁	25–30 minutes	All levels
	—— Interactive Tutor Self-Assessment CD-ROM 💿	20–30 minutes	All levels
	—— ExamView® Pro Testmaker CD-ROM 💿	15–20 minutes	All levels
	—— History Online Activity 🔌	15–20 minutes	All levels
	Reteach		
	—— Reteaching Activity 10–3, TCR 📁	15–20 minutes	ELL, L1
	—— Reading Essentials and Study Guide 10–3, TCR 📁	25–35 minutes	ELL, L1
	—— Take-Home Review Activity 10, TCR 📁	10–15 minutes	All levels
	—— MindJogger Videoquiz, Chapter 10 💿 📼	20–25 minutes	All levels
	Enrich		
	—— Enrichment Activity 10–3, TCR 📁	10–15 minutes	L2, L3
	CLOSE MENU		
	—— Close, TWE, p. 327	10–15 minutes	All levels

See Optional Resources menu on page viii.

Jacksonian Democracy

Section 1 *(pp. 334–339)*

LOCAL OBJECTIVES	TWE—Teacher Wraparound Edition TCR—Teacher Classroom Resources
	📁 Blackline Master 🖊 Transparency 💿 CD-ROM 📀 DVD 📙 Poster
	🎵 Music Program 🔊 Audio Program 📼 Videocassette 🖱 Internet Resources

OBJECTIVES

1. Explain why the nation's sixth president was chosen by the House of Representatives.
2. Identify the changes President Jackson brought to the American political system.

	FOCUS MENU	**SUGGESTED TIME RANGES**	**SUGGESTED LEVEL**
	—— Daily Focus Skills Transparency 11–1, TCR 🖊 📁	5–10 minutes	L1
	—— Preteaching Vocabulary, TWE, p. 334	5–10 minutes	All levels
	—— History Online Chapter 11 Overview 🖱	15–20 minutes	All levels
	—— Audio Program Chapter 11 🔊	20–25 minutes	All levels

	TEACH MENU		
	Guided Practice		
	—— Time Line Activity, TWE, p. 333	5–10 minutes	All levels
	—— Activity, TWE, p. 335	5–10 minutes	L1
	—— Cooperative Learning Activity, TWE, p. 335	40–60 minutes	ELL, L1
	—— Meeting Special Needs, TWE, p. 336	25–35 minutes	L1
	—— Interdisciplinary Connections Activity, TWE, p. 337	20–30 minutes	L2
	—— Critical Thinking Activity, TWE, p. 338	20–25 minutes	L3
	—— Graphic Organizer Transparency Strategy and Activity 11, TCR 🖊 📁	15–20 minutes	L2
	—— Why It Matters Chapter Transparency Strategy and Activity 11, TCR 🖊 📁	25–30 minutes	All levels
	Independent Practice		
	—— Guided Reading Activity 11–1, TCR 📁	15–20 minutes	ELL, L1
	—— Reading and Study Skills Foldable, p. 333	10–15 minutes	All levels

	ASSESS MENU		
	Evaluate		
	—— Section Quiz 11–1, TCR 📁	10–15 minutes	All levels
	—— Interactive Tutor Self-Assessment CD-ROM 💿	20–30 minutes	All levels
	—— ExamView® Pro Testmaker CD-ROM 💿	15–20 minutes	All levels
	Reteach		
	—— Reteaching Activity 11–1, TCR 📁	15–20 minutes	ELL, L1
	—— Reading Essentials and Study Guide 11–1, TCR 📁	25–35 minutes	ELL, L1
	Enrich		
	—— Enrichment Activity 11–1, TCR 📁	10–15 minutes	L2, L3

	CLOSE MENU		
	—— Close, TWE, p. 339	10–15 minutes	All levels

See Optional Resources menu on page viii.

Conflicts Over Land

Section 2 *(pp. 341–345)*

LOCAL OBJECTIVES	TWE—Teacher Wraparound Edition TCR—Teacher Classroom Resources Blackline Master Transparency CD-ROM DVD Poster Music Program Audio Program Videocassette Internet Resources		
	OBJECTIVES **1.** Understand how Native Americans were forced off their lands in the Southeast. **2.** Explain how President Jackson defied the Supreme Court.		
	FOCUS MENU	**SUGGESTED TIME RANGES**	**SUGGESTED LEVEL**
	—— Daily Focus Skills Transparency 11–2, TCR	5–10 minutes	L1
	—— Preteaching Vocabulary, TWE, p. 341	5–10 minutes	All levels
	—— Audio Program Chapter 11	20–25 minutes	All levels
	TEACH MENU **Guided Practice**		
	—— Activity, TWE, p. 342	5–10 minutes	L1
	—— Cooperative Learning Activity, TWE, p. 342	40–60 minutes	ELL, L1
	—— Meeting Special Needs, TWE, p. 343	25–35 minutes	L1
	—— Interdisciplinary Connections Activity, TWE, p. 344	20–30 minutes	L2
	—— Graphic Organizer Transparencies Strategies and Activities, TCR	20–25 minutes	All levels
	Independent Practice		
	—— Guided Reading Activity 11–2, TCR	15–20 minutes	ELL, L1
	ASSESS MENU **Evaluate**		
	—— Section Quiz 11–2, TCR	10–15 minutes	All levels
	—— Interactive Tutor Self-Assessment CD-ROM	20–30 minutes	All levels
	—— ExamView® Pro Testmaker CD-ROM	15–20 minutes	All levels
	—— History Online Activity	15–20 minutes	All levels
	Reteach		
	—— Reteaching Activity 11–2, TCR	15–20 minutes	ELL, L1
	—— Reading Essentials and Study Guide 11–2, TCR	25–35 minutes	ELL, L1
	Enrich		
	—— Enrichment Activity 11–2, TCR	10–15 minutes	L2, L3
	—— Linking Past and Present Activity 11, TCR	15–20 minutes	All levels
	CLOSE MENU		
	—— Close, TWE, p. 345	10–15 minutes	All levels

See Optional Resources menu on page viii.

Grade _____ Class(es) _____ Date _____ M Tu W Th F

Teacher's Name _____ Date _____

Jackson and the Bank
Section 3 (pp. 348–351)

LOCAL OBJECTIVES	TWE—Teacher Wraparound Edition TCR—Teacher Classroom Resources
	📁 Blackline Master 🔦 Transparency 💿 CD-ROM 💿 DVD 🖼 Poster
	🎵 Music Program 🔊 Audio Program 📼 Videocassette 🖱 Internet Resources

OBJECTIVES

1. Examine the reasons why Jackson wanted to destroy the Bank of the United States.

2. Understand why the Whigs came to power in 1840.

FOCUS MENU	SUGGESTED TIME RANGES	SUGGESTED LEVEL
—— Daily Focus Skills Transparency 11–3, TCR 🔦 📁	5–10 minutes	L1
—— Vocabulary PuzzleMaker CD-ROM 💿	5–10 minutes	All levels
—— Audio Program Chapter 11 🔊	20–25 minutes	All levels

TEACH MENU

Guided Practice

—— Activity, TWE, p. 349	5–10 minutes	ELL, L1
—— Cooperative Learning Activity, TWE, p. 349	40–60 minutes	ELL, L1
—— Meeting Special Needs, TWE, p. 350	25–35 minutes	L1
—— Graphic Organizer Transparencies	20–25 minutes	All levels
Strategies and Activities, TCR 🔦 📁		

Independent Practice

—— Guided Reading Activity 11–3, TCR 📁	15–20 minutes	ELL, L1
—— Vocabulary Activity 11, TCR 📁	20–30 minutes	All levels
—— Chapter Skills Activity 11, TCR 📁	40–60 minutes	L2, L3
—— Critical Thinking Activity 11, TCR 📁	15–20 minutes	L1
—— Geography and History Activity 11, TCR 📁	10–15 minutes	All levels
—— Time Line Activity 11, TCR 📁	15–20 minutes	All levels

ASSESS MENU

Evaluate

—— Section Quiz 11–3, TCR 📁	10–15 minutes	All levels
—— Performance Assessment Activity 11, TCR 📁	25–30 minutes	All levels
—— Interactive Tutor Self-Assessment CD-ROM 💿	20–30 minutes	All levels
—— ExamView® Pro Testmaker CD-ROM 💿	15–20 minutes	All levels

Reteach

—— Reteaching Activity 11–3, TCR 📁	15–20 minutes	ELL, L1
—— Reading Essentials and Study Guide 11–3, TCR 📁	25–35 minutes	ELL, L1
—— Take-Home Review Activity 11, TCR 📼	10–15 minutes	All levels
—— MindJogger Videoquiz, Chapter 11 💿 📼	20–25 minutes	All levels

Enrich

—— Enrichment Activity 11–3, TCR 📁	10–15 minutes	L2, L3
—— Primary Source Reading 11, TCR 📁	20–30 minutes	All levels

CLOSE MENU

—— Close, TWE, p. 351	10–15 minutes	All levels

See Optional Resources menu on page viii.

The Oregon Country

Section 1 *(pp. 356–360)*

LOCAL OBJECTIVES	TWE—Teacher Wraparound Edition TCR—Teacher Classroom Resources		
	🗁 Blackline Master 🖎 Transparency ⊙ CD-ROM ⊙ DVD ⬛ Poster		
	🎵 Music Program ⓐ Audio Program 📼 Videocassette ⬸ Internet Resources		

	OBJECTIVES 1. Explain why large numbers of settlers headed for the Oregon country. 2. Understand how the idea of Manifest Destiny contributed to the nation's growth.		
	FOCUS MENU	**SUGGESTED TIME RANGES**	**SUGGESTED LEVEL**
	—— Daily Focus Skills Transparency 12–1, TCR 🖎 🗁	5–10 minutes	L1
	—— Preteaching Vocabulary, TWE, p. 356	5–10 minutes	All levels
	—— History Online Chapter 12 Overview ⬸	15–20 minutes	All levels
	—— Audio Program Chapter 12 ⓐ	20–25 minutes	All levels
	TEACH MENU **Guided Practice**		
	—— Time Line Activity, TWE, p. 355	5–10 minutes	All levels
	—— Activity, TWE, p. 357	5–10 minutes	L1
	—— Cooperative Learning Activity, TWE, p. 357	40–60 minutes	ELL, L1
	—— Meeting Special Needs, TWE, p. 358	25–35 minutes	L1
	—— Interdisciplinary Connections Activity, TWE, p. 359	20–30 minutes	L2
	—— Graphic Organizer Transparencies Strategies and Activities, TCR 🖎 🗁	20–25 minutes	All levels
	Independent Practice		
	—— Guided Reading Activity 12–1, TCR 🗁	15–20 minutes	ELL, L1
	—— Reading and Study Skills Foldable, p. 355	10–15 minutes	All levels
	ASSESS MENU **Evaluate**		
	—— Section Quiz 12–1, TCR 🗁	10–15 minutes	All levels
	—— Interactive Tutor Self-Assessment CD-ROM ⊙	20–30 minutes	All levels
	—— ExamView® Pro Testmaker CD-ROM ⊙	15–20 minutes	All levels
	Reteach		
	—— Reteaching Activity 12–1, TCR 🗁	15–20 minutes	ELL, L1
	—— Reading Essentials and Study Guide 12–1, TCR 🗁	25–35 minutes	ELL, L1
	Enrich		
	—— Enrichment Activity 12–1, TCR 🗁	10–15 minutes	L2, L3
	—— Linking Past and Present Activity 12, TCR 🗁	15–20 minutes	All levels
	CLOSE MENU		
	—— Close, TWE, p. 360	10–15 minutes	All levels

See Optional Resources menu on page viii.

Grade _____ Class(es) _____ Date _____ M Tu W Th F

Teacher's Name _____ Date _____

Independence for Texas

Section 2 *(pp. 362–368)*

LOCAL OBJECTIVES	TWE—Teacher Wraparound Edition TCR—Teacher Classroom Resources 📁 Blackline Master ⬛ Transparency 💿 CD-ROM 📀 DVD 📱 Poster 🎵 Music Program 🎧 Audio Program 📼 Videocassette 🖱 Internet Resources

	OBJECTIVES
	1. Understand why problems arose between the Mexican government and American settlers in Texas.
	2. Describe how Texas achieved independence from Mexico and later became a state.

	FOCUS MENU	**SUGGESTED TIME RANGES**	**SUGGESTED LEVEL**
	—— Daily Focus Skills Transparency 12–2, TCR ⬛ 📁	5–10 minutes	L1
	—— Preteaching Vocabulary, TWE, p. 362	5–10 minutes	All levels
	—— Audio Program Chapter 12 🎧	20–25 minutes	All levels

	TEACH MENU		
	Guided Practice		
	—— Activity, TWE, p. 363	5–10 minutes	L1
	—— Cooperative Learning Activity, TWE, p. 363	40–60 minutes	ELL, L1
	—— Meeting Special Needs, TWE, p. 364	25–35 minutes	L1
	—— Interdisciplinary Connections Activity, TWE, p. 365	20–30 minutes	L2
	—— Critical Thinking Activity, TWE, p. 366	20–25 minutes	L2
	—— Extending the Content, TWE, p. 367	5–10 minutes	All levels
	—— Graphic Organizer Transparency Strategy and Activity 12, TCR ⬛ 📁	15–20 minutes	L2
	Independent Practice		
	—— Guided Reading Activity 12–2, TCR 📁	15–20 minutes	ELL, L1

	ASSESS MENU		
	Evaluate		
	—— Section Quiz 12–2, TCR 📁	10–15 minutes	All levels
	—— Interactive Tutor Self-Assessment CD-ROM 💿	20–30 minutes	All levels
	—— ExamView® Pro Testmaker CD-ROM 💿	15–20 minutes	All levels
	—— History Online Activity 🖱	15–20 minutes	All levels
	Reteach		
	—— Reteaching Activity 12–2, TCR 📁	15–20 minutes	ELL, L1
	—— Reading Essentials and Study Guide 12–2, TCR 📁	25–35 minutes	ELL, L1
	Enrich		
	—— Enrichment Activity 12–2, TCR 📁	10–15 minutes	L2, L3

	CLOSE MENU		
	—— Close, TWE, p. 368	10–15 minutes	All levels

See Optional Resources menu on page viii.

Grade _____ Class(es) _____ Date _____ M Tu W Th F

Teacher's Name _____ Date _____

War with Mexico
Section 3 *(pp. 369–374)*

LOCAL OBJECTIVES	TWE—Teacher Wraparound Edition TCR—Teacher Classroom Resources		

TWE—Teacher Wraparound Edition   TCR—Teacher Classroom Resources
📁 Blackline Master   ♨ Transparency   ◉ CD-ROM   ◉ DVD   📕 Poster
🎏 Music Program   ◎ Audio Program   📼 Videocassette   ☞ Internet Resources

OBJECTIVES
1. Explain why Americans began to settle in the Southwest.
2. Describe how the United States acquired New Mexico and California.

FOCUS MENU	SUGGESTED TIME RANGES	SUGGESTED LEVEL
____ Daily Focus Skills Transparency 12–3, TCR ♨ 📁	5–10 minutes	L1
____ Preteaching Vocabulary, TWE, p. 369	5–10 minutes	All levels
____ Audio Program Chapter 12 ◎	20–25 minutes	All levels

TEACH MENU
Guided Practice

____ Activity, TWE, p. 370	5–10 minutes	L1
____ Cooperative Learning Activity, TWE, p. 370	40–60 minutes	ELL, L1
____ Meeting Special Needs, TWE, p. 371	25–35 minutes	L1
____ Interdisciplinary Connections Activity, TWE, p. 372	20–30 minutes	L2
____ Critical Thinking Activity, TWE, p. 373	20–25 minutes	L2
____ Graphic Organizer Transparencies Strategies and Activities, TCR ♨ 📁	20–25 minutes	All levels

Independent Practice

____ Guided Reading Activity 12–3, TCR 📁	15–20 minutes	ELL, L1

ASSESS MENU
Evaluate

____ Section Quiz 12–3, TCR 📁	10–15 minutes	All levels
____ Interactive Tutor Self-Assessment CD-ROM ◉	20–30 minutes	All levels
____ ExamView® Pro Testmaker CD-ROM ◉	15–20 minutes	All levels

Reteach

____ Reteaching Activity 12–3, TCR 📁	15–20 minutes	ELL, L1
____ Reading Essentials and Study Guide 12–3, TCR 📁	25–35 minutes	ELL, L1

Enrich

____ Enrichment Activity 12–3, TCR 📁	10–15 minutes	L2, L3

CLOSE MENU

____ Close, TWE, p. 374	10–15 minutes	All levels

See Optional Resources menu on page viii.

Grade _____ Class(es) _____ Date _____ M Tu W Th F

Teacher's Name _____ Date _____

New Settlers in California and Utah Section 4 (pp. 375–378)

LOCAL OBJECTIVES	TWE—Teacher Wraparound Edition TCR—Teacher Classroom Resources 📁 Blackline Master 🔨 Transparency 💿 CD-ROM 📀 DVD 📱 Poster 🎵 Music Program 🎧 Audio Program 📼 Videocassette 〰 Internet Resources

	OBJECTIVES
	1. Understand how the hopes of getting rich quick drew thousands of people to California.
	2. Describe how the search for religious freedom led to the settlement of Utah.

	FOCUS MENU	**SUGGESTED TIME RANGES**	**SUGGESTED LEVEL**
	—— Daily Focus Skills Transparency 12–4, TCR 🔨 📁	5–10 minutes	L1
	—— Vocabulary PuzzleMaker CD-ROM 💿	5–10 minutes	All levels
	—— Audio Program Chapter 12 🎧	20–25 minutes	All levels

	TEACH MENU		
	Guided Practice		
	—— Activity, TWE, p. 376	5–10 minutes	L2
	—— Cooperative Learning Activity, TWE, p. 376	40–60 minutes	L3
	—— Meeting Special Needs, TWE, p. 377	25–35 minutes	L1
	—— Graphic Organizer Transparencies Strategies and Activities, TCR 🔨 📁	20–25 minutes	All levels
	—— Why It Matters Chapter Transparency Strategy and Activity 12, TCR 🔨 📁	25–30 minutes	All levels
	Independent Practice		
	—— Guided Reading Activity 12–4, TCR 📁	15–20 minutes	ELL, L1
	—— Vocabulary Activity 12, TCR 📁	20–30 minutes	All levels
	—— Chapter Skills Activity 12, TCR 📁	40–60 minutes	L1
	—— Critical Thinking Activity 12, TCR 📁	15–20 minutes	L2, L3
	—— Geography and History Activity 12, TCR 📁	10–15 minutes	All levels
	—— Time Line Activity 12, TCR 📁	10–15 minutes	All levels

	ASSESS MENU		
	Evaluate		
	—— Section Quiz 12–4, TCR 📁	10–15 minutes	All levels
	—— Performance Assessment Activity 12, TCR 📁	25–30 minutes	All levels
	—— Interactive Tutor Self-Assessment CD-ROM 💿	20–30 minutes	All levels
	—— ExamView® Pro Testmaker CD-ROM 💿	15–20 minutes	All levels
	Reteach		
	—— Reteaching Activity 12–4, TCR 📁	15–20 minutes	ELL, L1
	—— Reading Essentials and Study Guide 12–4, TCR 📁	25–35 minutes	ELL, L1
	—— Take-Home Review Activity 12, TCR 📁	10–15 minutes	All levels
	—— MindJogger Videoquiz, Chapter 12 📀 📼	20–25 minutes	All levels
	Enrich		
	—— Enrichment Activity 12–4, TCR 📁	10–15 minutes	L2, L3
	—— Primary Source Reading 12, TCR 📁	20–30 minutes	All levels

	CLOSE MENU		
	—— Close, TWE, p. 378	10–15 minutes	All levels

See Optional Resources menu on page viii.

The North's Economy

Section 1 *(pp. 386–390)*

LOCAL OBJECTIVES	TWE—Teacher Wraparound Edition TCR—Teacher Classroom Resources 📁 Blackline Master ✋ Transparency 💿 CD-ROM ⊙ DVD 📕 Poster 🎵 Music Program ⊚ Audio Program 📼 Videocassette ⬱ Internet Resources

	OBJECTIVES		
	1. Understand how advances in technology shaped the economy of the North.		
	2. Explain how new kinds of transportation and communication spurred economic growth.		

	FOCUS MENU	**SUGGESTED TIME RANGES**	**SUGGESTED LEVEL**
	—— Daily Focus Skills Transparency 13–1, TCR ✋ 📁	5–10 minutes	L1
	—— Preteaching Vocabulary, TWE, p. 386	5–10 minutes	All levels
	—— History Online Chapter 13 Overview ⬱	15–20 minutes	All levels
	—— Audio Program Chapter 13 ⊚	20-25 minutes	All levels

	TEACH MENU		
	Guided Practice		
	—— Time Line Activity, TWE, p. 385	5–10 minutes	All levels
	—— Activity, TWE, p. 387	5–10 minutes	L1
	—— Cooperative Learning Activity, TWE, p. 387	40–60 minutes	ELL, L1
	—— Meeting Special Needs, TWE, p. 388	25–35 minutes	L1
	—— Interdisciplinary Connections Activity, TWE, p. 389	20–30 minutes	L2
	—— Graphic Organizer Transparency Strategy and Activity 13, TCR ✋ 📁	15–20 minutes	L2
	—— Why It Matters Chapter Transparency Strategy and Activity 13, TCR ✋ 📁	25–30 minutes	All levels
	Independent Practice		
	—— Guided Reading Activity 13–1, TCR 📁	15–20 minutes	ELL, L1
	—— Reading and Study Skills Foldable, p. 385	10–15 minutes	All levels

	ASSESS MENU		
	Evaluate		
	—— Section Quiz 13–1, TCR 📁	10–15 minutes	All levels
	—— Interactive Tutor Self-Assessment CD-ROM 💿	20–30 minutes	All levels
	—— ExamView® Pro Testmaker CD-ROM 💿	15–20 minutes	All levels
	Reteach		
	—— Reteaching Activity 13–1, TCR 📁	15–20 minutes	ELL, L1
	—— Reading Essentials and Study Guide 13–1, TCR 📁	25–35 minutes	ELL, L1
	Enrich		
	—— Enrichment Activity 13–1, TCR 📁	10–15 minutes	L2, L3
	—— Linking Past and Present Activity 13, TCR 📁	15–20 minutes	All levels

	CLOSE MENU		
	—— Close, TWE, p. 390	10–15 minutes	All levels

See Optional Resources menu on page viii.

Grade _____ Class(es) _____ Date _____ M Tu W Th F

Teacher's Name _____ Date _____

The North's People

Section 2 (pp. 391–395)

LOCAL OBJECTIVES	TWE—Teacher Wraparound Edition 　　TCR—Teacher Classroom Resources 📁 Blackline Master 　🏳 Transparency 　💿 CD-ROM 　💿 DVD 　📙 Poster 🎵 Music Program 　🎧 Audio Program 　📼 Videocassette 　🖰 Internet Resources

OBJECTIVES
1. Summarize how working conditions in industries changed.
2. Compare and contrast how immigration affected American economic, political, and cultural life.

		SUGGESTED TIME RANGES	SUGGESTED LEVEL
FOCUS MENU			
——	Daily Focus Skills Transparency 13–2, TCR 🏳 📁	5–10 minutes	L1
——	Preteaching Vocabulary, TWE, p. 391	5–10 minutes	All levels
——	Audio Program Chapter 13 🎧	20–25 minutes	All levels
TEACH MENU			
Guided Practice			
——	Activity, TWE, p. 392	5–10 minutes	L2
——	Cooperative Learning Activity, TWE, p. 392	40–60 minutes	L2
——	Meeting Special Needs, TWE, p. 393	25–35 minutes	L1
——	Interdisciplinary Connections Activity, TWE, p. 394	20–30 minutes	L2
——	Graphic Organizer Transparencies Strategies and Activities, TCR 🏳 📁	20–25 minutes	All levels
Independent Practice			
——	Guided Reading Activity 13–2, TCR 📁	15–20 minutes	ELL, L1
ASSESS MENU			
Evaluate			
——	Section Quiz 13–2, TCR 📁	10–15 minutes	All levels
——	Interactive Tutor Self-Assessment CD-ROM 💿	20–30 minutes	All levels
——	ExamView® Pro Testmaker CD-ROM 💿	15–20 minutes	All levels
Reteach			
——	Reteaching Activity 13–2, TCR 📁	15–20 minutes	ELL, L1
——	Reading Essentials and Study Guide 13–2, TCR 📁	25–35 minutes	ELL, L1
Enrich			
——	Enrichment Activity 13–2, TCR 📁	10–15 minutes	L2, L3
——	Primary Source Reading 13, TCR 📁	20–30 minutes	All levels
CLOSE MENU			
——	Close, TWE, p. 395	10–15 minutes	All levels

See Optional Resources menu on page viii.

Southern Cotton Kingdom
Section 3 *(pp. 397–400)*

LOCAL OBJECTIVES	TWE—Teacher Wraparound Edition TCR—Teacher Classroom Resources
	📁 Blackline Master ✋ Transparency ● CD-ROM ◉ DVD 📕 Poster
	🏴 Music Program 🎧 Audio Program 📼 Videocassette 🖱 Internet Resources

OBJECTIVES
1. Explore how settlement expanded in the South.
2. Determine why the economy of the South relied on agriculture.

	FOCUS MENU	SUGGESTED TIME RANGES	SUGGESTED LEVEL
	—— Daily Focus Skills Transparency 13–3, TCR ✋ 📁	5–10 minutes	L1
	—— Preteaching Vocabulary, TWE, p. 397	5–10 minutes	All levels
	—— Audio Program Chapter 13 🎧	20–25 minutes	All levels

	TEACH MENU		
	Guided Practice		
	—— Activity, TWE, p. 398	5–10 minutes	L1
	—— Cooperative Learning Activity, TWE, p. 398	40–60 minutes	ELL, L2
	—— Meeting Special Needs, TWE, p. 399	25–35 minutes	L1
	—— Graphic Organizer Transparencies Strategies and Activities, TCR ✋ 📁	20–25 minutes	All levels
	Independent Practice		
	—— Guided Reading Activity 13–3, TCR 📁	15–20 minutes	ELL, L1

	ASSESS MENU		
	Evaluate		
	—— Section Quiz 13–3, TCR 📁	10–15 minutes	All levels
	—— Interactive Tutor Self-Assessment CD-ROM ●	20–30 minutes	All levels
	—— ExamView® Pro Testmaker CD-ROM ●	15–20 minutes	All levels
	Reteach		
	—— Reteaching Activity 13–3, TCR 📁	15–20 minutes	ELL, L1
	—— Reading Essentials and Study Guide 13–3, TCR 📁	25–35 minutes	ELL, L1
	Enrich		
	—— Enrichment Activity 13–3, TCR 📁	10–15 minutes	L2, L3

	CLOSE MENU		
	—— Close, TWE, p. 400	10–15 minutes	All levels

See Optional Resources menu on page viii.

Grade _____ Class(es) _____ Date _____ M Tu W Th F

Teacher's Name _____ Date _____

The South's People   Section 4 (pp. 401–407)

LOCAL OBJECTIVES	TWE—Teacher Wraparound Edition TCR—Teacher Classroom Resources 📁 Blackline Master 🖌 Transparency 💿 CD-ROM ⊙ DVD 🖥 Poster 🎵 Music Program 🎧 Audio Program 📼 Videocassette 🖱 Internet Resources		
	OBJECTIVES **1.** Describe what life was like on Southern plantations. **2.** Understand how enslaved workers maintained strong family and cultural ties.		
	FOCUS MENU	**SUGGESTED TIME RANGES**	**SUGGESTED LEVEL**
	—— Daily Focus Skills Transparency 13–4, TCR 🖌 📁	5–10 minutes	L1
	—— Vocabulary PuzzleMaker CD-ROM 💿	5–10 minutes	All levels
	—— Audio Program Chapter 13 🎧	20–25 minutes	All levels
	TEACH MENU **Guided Practice**		
	—— Activity, TWE, p. 402	5–10 minutes	L2
	—— Cooperative Learning Activity, TWE, p. 402	40–60 minutes	L2
	—— Meeting Special Needs, TWE, p. 403	25–35 minutes	L1
	—— Interdisciplinary Connections Activity, TWE, p. 404	20–30 minutes	L1
	—— Critical Thinking Activity, TWE, p. 405	20–25 minutes	L2
	—— Extending the Content, TWE, p. 406	5–10 minutes	All levels
	—— Graphic Organizer Transparencies Strategies and Activities, TCR 🖌 📁	20–25 minutes	All levels
	Independent Practice		
	—— Guided Reading Activity 13–4, TCR 📁	15–20 minutes	ELL, L1
	—— Vocabulary Activity 13, TCR 📁	20–30 minutes	All levels
	—— Chapter Skills Activity 13, TCR 📁	20–30 minutes	All levels
	—— Critical Thinking Activity 13, TCR 📁	20–30 minutes	L1
	—— Geography and History Activity 13, TCR 📁	15–20 minutes	All levels
	—— Time Line Activity 13, TCR 📁	10–15 minutes	All levels
	ASSESS MENU **Evaluate**		
	—— Section Quiz 13–4, TCR 📁	10–15 minutes	All levels
	—— Performance Assessment Activity 13, TCR 📁	25–30 minutes	All levels
	—— Interactive Tutor Self-Assessment CD-ROM 💿	20–30 minutes	All levels
	—— ExamView® Pro Testmaker CD-ROM 💿	15–20 minutes	All levels
	—— History Online Activity 🖱	15–20 minutes	All levels
	Reteach		
	—— Reteaching Activity 13–4, TCR 📁	15–20 minutes	ELL, L1
	—— Reading Essentials and Study Guide 13–4, TCR 📁	25–35 minutes	ELL, L1
	—— Take-Home Review Activity 13, TCR 📁	10–15 minutes	All levels
	—— MindJogger Videoquiz, Chapter 13 ⊙ 📼	20–25 minutes	All levels
	Enrich		
	—— Enrichment Activity 13–4, TCR 📁	10–15 minutes	L2, L3
	CLOSE MENU		
	—— Close, TWE, p. 407	10–15 minutes	All levels

See Optional Resources menu on page viii.

Social Reform

Section 1 *(pp. 412–415)*

LOCAL OBJECTIVES	TWE—Teacher Wraparound Edition TCR—Teacher Classroom Resources 📁 Blackline Master 🖲 Transparency 🔘 CD-ROM ⊙ DVD 📱 Poster 🎵 Music Program 🔊 Audio Program 📼 Videocassette 🖇 Internet Resources		
	OBJECTIVES **1.** Understand how religious and philosophical ideas inspired various reform movements. **2.** Explain why educational reformers thought all citizens should attend school.		
	FOCUS MENU	**SUGGESTED TIME RANGES**	**SUGGESTED LEVEL**
	____ Daily Focus Skills Transparency 14–1, TCR 🖲 📁	5–10 minutes	L1
	____ Preteaching Vocabulary, TWE, p. 412	5–10 minutes	All levels
	____ History Online Chapter 14 Overview 🖇	15–20 minutes	All levels
	____ Audio Program Chapter 14 🔊	20–25 minutes	All levels
	TEACH MENU **Guided Practice**		
	____ Time Line Activity, TWE, p. 411	15–20 minutes	All levels
	____ Activity, TWE, p. 413	5–10 minutes	L1
	____ Cooperative Learning Activity, TWE, p. 413	40–60 minutes	L3
	____ Meeting Special Needs, TWE, p. 414	25–35 minutes	L1
	____ Graphic Organizer Transparency Strategy and Activity 14, TCR 🖲 📁	15–20 minutes	L2
	____ American Art and Architecture 🖲 📁	25–30 minutes	All levels
	Independent Practice		
	____ Guided Reading Activity 14–1, TCR 📁	15–20 minutes	ELL, L1
	____ Reading and Study Skills Foldable, p. 411	10–15 minutes	All levels
	ASSESS MENU **Evaluate**		
	____ Section Quiz 14–1, TCR 📁	10–15 minutes	All levels
	____ Interactive Tutor Self-Assessment CD-ROM 🔘	20–30 minutes	All levels
	____ ExamView® Pro Testmaker CD-ROM 🔘	15–20 minutes	All levels
	Reteach		
	____ Reteaching Activity 14–1, TCR 📁	15–20 minutes	ELL, L1
	____ Reading Essentials and Study Guide 14–1, TCR 📁	25–35 minutes	ELL, L1
	Enrich		
	____ Enrichment Activity 14–1, TCR 📁	10–15 minutes	L2, L3
	____ Linking Past and Present Activity 14, TCR 📁	15–20 minutes	All levels
	CLOSE MENU ____ Close, TWE, p. 415	10–15 minutes	All levels

See Optional Resources menu on page viii.

The Abolitionists

Section 2 *(pp. 418–424)*

LOCAL OBJECTIVES	TWE—Teacher Wraparound Edition TCR—Teacher Classroom Resources 📁 Blackline Master 🔥 Transparency 💿 CD-ROM 💿 DVD 📋 Poster 🎵 Music Program 🔊 Audio Program 📼 Videocassette 🖱 Internet Resources

	OBJECTIVES **1.** Describe the ways some Americans worked to eliminate slavery. **2.** Explore the reasons why many Americans feared the end of slavery.		

	FOCUS MENU	**SUGGESTED TIME RANGES**	**SUGGESTED LEVEL**
	—— Daily Focus Skills Transparency 14–2, TCR 🔥 📁	5–10 minutes	L1
	—— Preteaching Vocabulary, TWE, p. 418	5–10 minutes	All levels
	—— Audio Program Chapter 14 🔊	20–25 minutes	All levels

	TEACH MENU		
	Guided Practice		
	—— Activity, TWE, p. 419	5–10 minutes	L1
	—— Cooperative Learning Activity, TWE, p. 419	40–60 minutes	ELL, L2
	—— Meeting Special Needs, TWE, p. 420	25–35 minutes	L1
	—— Interdisciplinary Connections Activity, TWE, p. 421	20–30 minutes	L2
	—— Critical Thinking Activity, TWE, p. 422	20–25 minutes	L2
	—— Extending the Content, TWE, p. 423	5–10 minutes	All levels
	—— Graphic Organizer Transparencies Strategies and Activities, TCR 🔥 📁	20–25 minutes	All levels
	Independent Practice		
	—— Guided Reading Activity 14–2, TCR 📁	15–20 minutes	ELL, L1

	ASSESS MENU		
	Evaluate		
	—— Section Quiz 14–2, TCR 📁	10–15 minutes	All levels
	—— Interactive Tutor Self-Assessment CD-ROM 💿	20–30 minutes	All levels
	—— ExamView® Pro Testmaker CD-ROM 💿	15–20 minutes	All levels
	—— History Online Activity 🖱	15–20 minutes	All levels
	Reteach		
	—— Reteaching Activity 14–2, TCR 📁	15–20 minutes	ELL, L1
	—— Reading Essentials and Study Guide 14–2, TCR 📁	25–35 minutes	ELL, L1
	Enrich		
	—— Enrichment Activity 14–2, TCR 📁	10–15 minutes	L2, L3

	CLOSE MENU		
	—— Close, TWE, p. 424	10–15 minutes	All levels

See Optional Resources menu on page viii.

The Women's Movement

Section 3 *(pp. 425–428)*

LOCAL OBJECTIVES	TWE—Teacher Wraparound Edition · TCR—Teacher Classroom Resources 📁 Blackline Master · 🖋 Transparency · 💿 CD-ROM · 💿 DVD · 📖 Poster 🎵 Music Program · 🔊 Audio Program · 📼 Videocassette · 〰 Internet Resources		
	OBJECTIVES **1.** Examine how the antislavery and the women's rights movements were related. **2.** Evaluate what progress women made toward equality during the 1800s.		
	FOCUS MENU	**SUGGESTED TIME RANGES**	**SUGGESTED LEVEL**
	____ Daily Focus Skills Transparency 14–3, TCR 🖋 📁	5–10 minutes	L1
	____ Vocabulary PuzzleMaker CD-ROM 💿	5–10 minutes	All levels
	____ Audio Program Chapter 14 🔊	20–25 minutes	All levels
	TEACH MENU **Guided Practice**		
	____ Activity, TWE, p. 426	5–10 minutes	L1
	____ Cooperative Learning Activity, TWE, p. 426	40–60 minutes	L2
	____ Meeting Special Needs, TWE, p. 427	25–35 minutes	L1
	____ Graphic Organizer Transparencies Strategies and Activities, TCR 🖋 📁	20–25 minutes	All levels
	____ Why It Matters Chapter Transparency Strategy and Activity 14, TCR 🖋 📁	25–30 minutes	All levels
	Independent Practice		
	____ Guided Reading Activity 14–3 TCR 📁	15–20 minutes	ELL, L1
	____ Vocabulary Activity 14, TCR 📁	20–30 minutes	All levels
	____ Chapter Skills Activity 14, TCR 📁	40–60 minutes	L1
	____ Critical Thinking Activity 14, TCR 📁	20–30 minutes	L1
	____ Geography and History Activity 14, TCR 📁	15–20 minutes	L1
	____ Time Line Activity 14, TCR 📁	10–15 minutes	All levels
	ASSESS MENU **Evaluate**		
	____ Section Quiz 14–3, TCR 📁	10–15 minutes	All levels
	____ Performance Assessment Activity 14, TCR 📁	25–30 minutes	All levels
	____ Interactive Tutor Self-Assessment CD-ROM 💿	20–30 minutes	All levels
	____ ExamView® Pro Testmaker CD-ROM 💿	15–20 minutes	All levels
	Reteach		
	____ Reteaching Activity 14–3, TCR 📁	15–20 minutes	ELL, L1
	____ Reading Essentials and Study Guide 14–3, TCR 📁	25–35 minutes	ELL, L1
	____ Take-Home Review Activity 14, TCR 📁	10–15 minutes	All levels
	____ MindJogger Videoquiz, Chapter 14 💿 📼	20–25 minutes	All levels
	Enrich		
	____ Enrichment Activity 14–3, TCR 📁	10–15 minutes	L2, L3
	____ Primary Source Reading 14, TCR 📁	20–30 minutes	All levels
	CLOSE MENU		
	____ Close, TWE, p. 428	10–15 minutes	All levels

See Optional Resources menu on page viii.

Grade _____   Class(es) _____   Date _____   M Tu W Th F

Teacher's Name _____   Date _____

REPRODUCIBLE LESSON PLAN 15–1

Slavery and the West

Section 1 (pp. 436–439)

LOCAL OBJECTIVES	TWE—Teacher Wraparound Edition TCR—Teacher Classroom Resources 📁 Blackline Master 🔦 Transparency 💿 CD-ROM 💿 DVD 📖 Poster 🎵 Music Program 🎧 Audio Program 📼 Videocassette ⌁ Internet Resources		
	OBJECTIVES **1.** Describe how the debate over slavery was related to the admission of new states. **2.** Understand what the Compromise of 1850 accomplished.		

	FOCUS MENU	**SUGGESTED TIME RANGES**	**SUGGESTED LEVEL**
	—— Daily Focus Skills Transparency 15–1, TCR 🔦 📁	5–10 minutes	L1
	—— Preteaching Vocabulary, TWE, p. 436	5–10 minutes	All levels
	—— History Online Chapter 15 Overview ⌁	15–20 minutes	All levels
	—— Audio Program Chapter 15 🎧	20–25 minutes	All levels

	TEACH MENU		
	Guided Practice		
	—— Time Line Activity, TWE, p. 435	15–20 minutes	L1
	—— Activity, TWE, p. 437	5–10 minutes	L2
	—— Cooperative Learning Activity, TWE, p. 437	40–60 minutes	L2
	—— Meeting Special Needs, TWE, p. 438	25–35 minutes	L1
	—— Graphic Organizer Transparencies Strategies and Activities, TCR 🔦 📁	20–25 minutes	All levels
	Independent Practice		
	—— Guided Reading Activity 15–1, TCR 📁	15–20 minutes	ELL, L1
	—— Reading and Study Skills Foldable, p. 435	10–15 minutes	All levels

	ASSESS MENU		
	Evaluate		
	—— Section Quiz 15–1, TCR 📁	10–15 minutes	All levels
	—— Interactive Tutor Self-Assessment CD-ROM 💿	20–30 minutes	All levels
	—— ExamView® Pro Testmaker CD-ROM 💿	15–20 minutes	All levels
	Reteach		
	—— Reteaching Activity 15–1, TCR 📁	15–20 minutes	ELL, L1
	—— Reading Essentials and Study Guide 15–1, TCR 📁	25–35 minutes	ELL, L1
	Enrich		
	—— Enrichment Activity 15–1, TCR 📁	10–15 minutes	L2, L3

	CLOSE MENU		
	—— Close, TWE, p. 439	10–15 minutes	All levels

See Optional Resources menu on page viii.

Grade _____ Class(es) _____ Date _____ M Tu W Th F

Teacher's Name _____ Date _____

A Nation Dividing   Section 2 *(pp. 441–444)*

LOCAL OBJECTIVES	TWE—Teacher Wraparound Edition TCR—Teacher Classroom Resources 📁 Blackline Master ⬆ Transparency 🔘 CD-ROM 🔘 DVD 📙 Poster 🏁 Music Program 🎧 Audio Program 📼 Videocassette 🔗 Internet Resources		
	OBJECTIVES **1.** Explain how the Fugitive Slave Act and the Kansas-Nebraska Act further divided the North and South. **2.** Describe how popular sovereignty led to violence.		
	FOCUS MENU	**SUGGESTED TIME RANGES**	**SUGGESTED LEVEL**
	____ Daily Focus Skills Transparency 15–2, TCR ⬆ 📁	5–10 minutes	L1
	____ Preteaching Vocabulary, TWE, p. 441	5–10 minutes	All levels
	____ Audio Program Chapter 15 🎧	20–25 minutes	All levels
	TEACH MENU **Guided Practice**		
	____ Activity, TWE, p. 442	5–10 minutes	L1
	____ Cooperative Learning Activity, TWE, p. 442	40–60 minutes	L3
	____ Meeting Special Needs, TWE, p. 443	25–35 minutes	L1
	____ Graphic Organizer Transparency Strategy and Activity 15, TCR ⬆ 📁	15–20 minutes	L2
	Independent Practice		
	____ Guided Reading Activity 15–2, TCR 📁	15–20 minutes	ELL, L1
	ASSESS MENU Evaluate		
	____ Section Quiz 15–2, TCR 📁	10–15 minutes	All levels
	____ Interactive Tutor Self-Assessment CD-ROM 🔘	20–30 minutes	All levels
	____ ExamView® Pro Testmaker CD-ROM 🔘	15–20 minutes	All levels
	Reteach		
	____ Reteaching Activity 15–2, TCR 📁	15–20 minutes	ELL, L1
	____ Reading Essentials and Study Guide 15–2, TCR 📁	25–35 minutes	ELL, L1
	Enrich		
	____ Enrichment Activity 15–2, TCR 📁	10–15 minutes	L2, L3
	____ Primary Source Reading 15, TCR 📁	20–30 minutes	All levels
	CLOSE MENU		
	____ Close, TWE, p. 444	10–15 minutes	All levels

See Optional Resources menu on page viii.

Challenges to Slavery

Section 3 *(pp. 445–448)*

LOCAL OBJECTIVES	TWE—Teacher Wraparound Edition 📁 Blackline Master 🔨 Transparency 🎵 Music Program 🔊 Audio Program	TCR—Teacher Classroom Resources 💿 CD-ROM 📀 DVD 📷 Poster 📼 Videocassette 🖱 Internet Resources		
	OBJECTIVES **1.** Understand why the Republican Party was formed. **2.** Describe how the *Dred Scott* decision, the Lincoln-Douglas debates, and John Brown's raid affected Americans.			
	FOCUS MENU		**SUGGESTED TIME RANGES**	**SUGGESTED LEVEL**
	—— Daily Focus Skills Transparency 15–3, TCR 🔨 📁		5–10 minutes	L1
	—— Preteaching Vocabulary, TWE, p. 445		5–10 minutes	All levels
	—— Audio Program Chapter 15 🔊		20–25 minutes	All levels
	TEACH MENU **Guided Practice**			
	—— Activity, TWE, p. 446		5–10 minutes	ELL, L1
	—— Cooperative Learning Activity, TWE, p. 446		40–60 minutes	L3
	—— Meeting Special Needs, TWE, p. 447		25–35 minutes	L1
	—— Graphic Organizer Transparencies Strategies and Activities, TCR 🔨 📁		20–25 minutes	All levels
	—— Why It Matters Chapter Transparency Strategy and Activity 15, TCR 🔨 📁		25–30 minutes	All levels
	Independent Practice			
	—— Guided Reading Activity 15–3, TCR 📁		15–20 minutes	ELL, L1
	ASSESS MENU **Evaluate**			
	—— Section Quiz 15–3, TCR 📁		10–15 minutes	All levels
	—— Interactive Tutor Self-Assessment CD-ROM 💿		20–30 minutes	All levels
	—— ExamView® Pro Testmaker CD-ROM 💿		15–20 minutes	All levels
	Reteach			
	—— Reteaching Activity 15–3, TCR 📁		15–20 minutes	ELL, L1
	—— Reading Essentials and Study Guide 15–3, TCR 📁		25–35 minutes	ELL, L1
	Enrich			
	—— Enrichment Activity 15–3, TCR 📁		10–15 minutes	L2, L3
	CLOSE MENU			
	—— Close, TWE, p. 448		10–15 minutes	All levels

See Optional Resources menu on page viii.

Secession and War　　Section 4 (pp. 449–453)

LOCAL OBJECTIVES	TWE—Teacher Wraparound Edition　　　TCR—Teacher Classroom Resources
	📁 Blackline Master　🖐 Transparency　　💿 CD-ROM　　🔘 DVD　　📗 Poster
	🎵 Music Program　　🔊 Audio Program　　📼 Videocassette　　🖐 Internet Resources

	OBJECTIVES
	1. Explain how the 1860 election led to the breakup of the Union.
	2. Understand why secession led to the Civil War.

	FOCUS MENU	**SUGGESTED TIME RANGES**	**SUGGESTED LEVEL**
	____ Daily Focus Skills Transparency 15–4, TCR 🖐 📁	5–10 minutes	L1
	____ Vocabulary PuzzleMaker CD-ROM 💿	5–10 minutes	All levels
	____ Audio Program Chapter 15 🔊	20–25 minutes	All levels

	TEACH MENU		
	Guided Practice		
	____ Activity, TWE, p. 450	5–10 minutes	L1
	____ Cooperative Learning Activity, TWE, p. 450	40–60 minutes	ELL, L1
	____ Meeting Special Needs, TWE, p. 451	25–35 minutes	L1
	____ Interdisciplinary Connections Activity, TWE, p. 452	20–30 minutes	L2
	____ Graphic Organizer Transparencies Strategies and Activities, TCR 🖐 📁	20–25 minutes	All levels
	Independent Practice		
	____ Guided Reading Activity 15–4 TCR 📁	15–20 minutes	ELL, L1
	____ Vocabulary Activity 15, TCR 📁	20–30 minutes	All levels
	____ Chapter Skills Activity 15, TCR 📁	15–20 minutes	L1
	____ Critical Thinking Activity 15, TCR 📁	10–15 minutes	L2
	____ Geography and History Activity 15, TCR 📁	10–15 minutes	All levels
	____ Time Line Activity 15, TCR 📁	10–15 minutes	All levels

	ASSESS MENU		
	Evaluate		
	____ Section Quiz 15–4, TCR 📁	10–15 minutes	All levels
	____ Performance Assessment Activity 15, TCR 📁	25–30 minutes	All levels
	____ Interactive Tutor Self-Assessment CD-ROM 💿	20–30 minutes	All levels
	____ ExamView® Pro Testmaker CD-ROM 💿	15–20 minutes	All levels
	____ History Online Activity 🖐	15–20 minutes	All levels
	Reteach		
	____ Reteaching Activity 15–4, TCR 📁	15–20 minutes	ELL, L1
	____ Reading Essentials and Study Guide 15–4, TCR 📁	25–35 minutes	ELL, L1
	____ Take-Home Review Activity 15, TCR 📁	10–15 minutes	All levels
	____ MindJogger Videoquiz, Chapter 15 🔘 📼	20–25 minutes	All levels
	Enrich		
	____ Enrichment Activity 15–4, TCR 📁	10–15 minutes	L2, L3
	____ Linking Past and Present Activity 15, TCR 📁	15–20 minutes	All levels

	CLOSE MENU		
	____ Close, TWE, p. 453	10–15 minutes	All levels

See Optional Resources menu on page viii.

The Two Sides

Section 1 (pp. 460–464)

LOCAL OBJECTIVES	TWE—Teacher Wraparound Edition TCR—Teacher Classroom Resources 📁 Blackline Master 🕹 Transparency 💿 CD-ROM ⊙ DVD 🖼 Poster 🎵 Music Program 🎧 Audio Program 📼 Videocassette ⌐ Internet Resources

	OBJECTIVES		
	1. Explain why the border states played an important part in the war.		
	2. Compare Northern and Southern populations, industries, resources, and war aims.		

	FOCUS MENU	**SUGGESTED TIME RANGES**	**SUGGESTED LEVEL**
	—— Daily Focus Skills Transparency 16–1, TCR 🕹 📁	5–10 minutes	L1
	—— Preteaching Vocabulary, TWE, p. 460	5–10 minutes	All levels
	—— History Online Chapter 16 Overview ⌐	15–20 minutes	All levels
	—— Audio Program Chapter 16 🎧	20–25 minutes	All levels

	TEACH MENU		
	Guided Practice		
	—— Time Line Activity, TWE, p. 459	5–10 minutes	All levels
	—— Activity, TWE, p. 461	5–10 minutes	L1
	—— Cooperative Learning Activity, TWE, p. 461	40–60 minutes	L2
	—— Meeting Special Needs, TWE, p. 462	25–35 minutes	L1
	—— Interdisciplinary Connections Activity, TWE, p. 463	20–30 minutes	L2
	—— Graphic Organizer Transparencies Strategies and Activities, TCR 🕹 📁	20–25 minutes	All levels
	—— Why It Matters Chapter Transparency Strategy and Activity 16, TCR 🕹 📁	25–30 minutes	All levels
	Independent Practice		
	—— Guided Reading Activity 16–1, TCR 📁	15–20 minutes	ELL, L1
	—— Reading and Study Skills Foldable, p. 459	10–15 minutes	All levels

	ASSESS MENU		
	Evaluate		
	—— Section Quiz 16–1, TCR 📁	10–15 minutes	All levels
	—— Interactive Tutor Self-Assessment CD-ROM 💿	20–30 minutes	All levels
	—— ExamView® Pro Testmaker CD-ROM 💿	15–20 minutes	All levels
	Reteach		
	—— Reteaching Activity 16–1, TCR 📁	15–20 minutes	ELL, L1
	—— Reading Essentials and Study Guide 16–1, TCR 📁	25–35 minutes	ELL, L1
	Enrich		
	—— Enrichment Activity 16–1, TCR 📁	10–15 minutes	L2, L3

	CLOSE MENU		
	—— Close, TWE, p. 464	10–15 minutes	All levels

See Optional Resources menu on page viii.

Early Years of the War
Section 2 *(pp. 466–472)*

LOCAL OBJECTIVES	TWE—Teacher Wraparound Edition TCR—Teacher Classroom Resources
	📁 Blackline Master ♠ Transparency ◎ CD-ROM ◉ DVD 📕 Poster
	🎵 Music Program 📻 Audio Program 📺 Videocassette 🖱 Internet Resources

OBJECTIVES

1. Identify Northern and Southern successes and failures in the early years of the war.
2. Explain how the North's naval blockade hurt the South.

FOCUS MENU	SUGGESTED TIME RANGES	SUGGESTED LEVEL
____ Daily Focus Skills Transparency 16–2, TCR ♠ 📁	5–10 minutes	L1
____ Preteaching Vocabulary, TWE, p. 466	5–10 minutes	All levels
____ Audio Program Chapter 16 📻	20–25 minutes	All levels

TEACH MENU
Guided Practice

____ Activity, TWE, p. 467	5–10 minutes	L1
____ Cooperative Learning Activity, TWE, p. 467	40–60 minutes	L2
____ Meeting Special Needs, TWE, p. 468	25–35 minutes	L1
____ Interdisciplinary Connections Activity, TWE, p. 469	20–30 minutes	ELL, L2
____ Critical Thinking Activity, TWE, p. 470	20–25 minutes	L2
____ Extending the Content, TWE, p. 471	5–10 minutes	All levels
____ Graphic Organizer Transparencies Strategies and Activities, TCR ♠ 📁	20–25 minutes	All levels

Independent Practice

____ Guided Reading Activity 16–2, TCR 📁	15–20 minutes	ELL, L1

ASSESS MENU
Evaluate

____ Section Quiz 16–2, TCR 📁	10–15 minutes	All levels
____ Interactive Tutor Self-Assessment CD-ROM ◎	20–30 minutes	All levels
____ ExamView® Pro Testmaker CD-ROM ◎	15–20 minutes	All levels
____ History Online Activity 🖱	15–20 minutes	All levels

Reteach

____ Reteaching Activity 16–2, TCR 📁	15–20 minutes	ELL, L1
____ Reading Essentials and Study Guide 16–2, TCR 📁	25–35 minutes	ELL, L1

Enrich

____ Enrichment Activity 16–2, TCR 📁	10–15 minutes	L2, L3
____ Primary Source Reading 16, TCR 📁	20–30 minutes	All levels

CLOSE MENU

____ Close, TWE, p. 472	10–15 minutes	All levels

See Optional Resources menu on page viii.

A Call for Freedom

Section 3 (*pp. 473–477*)

LOCAL OBJECTIVES	TWE—Teacher Wraparound Edition TCR—Teacher Classroom Resources
	📁 Blackline Master 🏷 Transparency 🔘 CD-ROM 💿 DVD 📕 Poster
	🎵 Music Program 🔊 Audio Program 📼 Videocassette 🔗 Internet Resources

	OBJECTIVES		
	1. Describe why Lincoln issued the Emancipation Proclamation.		
	2. Understand the role that African Americans played in the Civil War.		
	FOCUS MENU	**SUGGESTED TIME RANGES**	**SUGGESTED LEVEL**
	—— Daily Focus Skills Transparency 16–3, TCR 🏷 📁	5–10 minutes	L1
	—— Preteaching Vocabulary, TWE, p. 473	5–10 minutes	All levels
	—— Audio Program Chapter 16 🔊	20–25 minutes	All levels
	TEACH MENU		
	Guided Practice		
	—— Activity, TWE, p. 474	5–10 minutes	L1
	—— Cooperative Learning Activity, TWE, p. 474	40–60 minutes	ELL, L1
	—— Meeting Special Needs, TWE, p. 475	25–35 minutes	L1
	—— Interdisciplinary Connections Activity, TWE, p. 476	20–30 minutes	L2
	—— Graphic Organizer Transparency Strategy and Activity 16, TCR 🏷 📁	15–20 minutes	L2
	Independent Practice		
	—— Guided Reading Activity 16–3, TCR 📁	15–20 minutes	ELL, L1
	ASSESS MENU		
	Evaluate		
	—— Section Quiz 16–3, TCR 📁	10–15 minutes	All levels
	—— Interactive Tutor Self-Assessment CD-ROM 🔘	20–30 minutes	All levels
	—— ExamView® Pro Testmaker CD-ROM 🔘	15–20 minutes	All levels
	Reteach		
	—— Reteaching Activity 16–3, TCR 📁	15–20 minutes	ELL, L1
	—— Reading Essentials and Study Guide 16–3, TCR 📁	25–35 minutes	ELL, L1
	Enrich		
	—— Enrichment Activity 16–3, TCR 📁	10–15 minutes	L2, L3
	CLOSE MENU		
	—— Close, TWE, p. 477	10–15 minutes	All levels

See Optional Resources menu on page viii.

Life During the Civil War

Section 4 *(pp. 478–483)*

LOCAL OBJECTIVES	TWE—Teacher Wraparound Edition TCR—Teacher Classroom Resources
	📁 Blackline Master 🖌 Transparency 💿 CD-ROM ⊙ DVD 🖥 Poster
	🏁 Music Program 🎧 Audio Program 📼 Videocassette ⟿ Internet Resources

	OBJECTIVES		
	1. Describe what life was like for soldiers during the Civil War.		
	2 Identify the role that women played in the war.		
	3. Compare how the war affected the economies of the North and the South.		

	FOCUS MENU	**SUGGESTED TIME RANGES**	**SUGGESTED LEVEL**
	—— Daily Focus Skills Transparency 16–4, TCR 🖌 📁	5–10 minutes	L1
	—— Preteaching Vocabulary, TWE, p. 478	5–10 minutes	All levels
	—— Audio Program Chapter 16 🎧	20–25 minutes	All levels

	TEACH MENU		
	Guided Practice		
	—— Activity, TWE, p. 479	5–10 minutes	L1
	—— Cooperative Learning Activity, TWE, p. 479	40–60 minutes	ELL, L1
	—— Meeting Special Needs, TWE, p. 480	25–35 minutes	L1
	—— Interdisciplinary Connections Activity, TWE, p. 481	20–30 minutes	ELL, L1
	—— Critical Thinking Activity, TWE, p. 482	20–25 minutes	L2
	—— Graphic Organizer Transparencies Strategies and Activities, TCR 🖌 📁	15–20 minutes	L2
	—— American Art and Architecture 🖌 📁	25–30 minutes	All levels
	Independent Practice		
	—— Guided Reading Activity 16–4, TCR 📁	15–20 minutes	ELL, L1

	ASSESS MENU		
	Evaluate		
	—— Section Quiz 16–4, TCR 📁	10–15 minutes	All levels
	—— Interactive Tutor Self-Assessment CD-ROM 💿	20–30 minutes	All levels
	—— ExamView® Pro Testmaker CD-ROM 💿	15–20 minutes	All levels
	Reteach		
	—— Reteaching Activity 16–4, TCR 📁	15–20 minutes	ELL, L1
	—— Reading Essentials and Study Guide 16–4, TCR 📁	25–35 minutes	ELL, L1
	Enrich		
	—— Enrichment Activity 16–4, TCR 📁	10–15 minutes	L2, L3
	—— Linking Past and Present Activity 16, TCR 📁	15–20 minutes	All levels

	CLOSE MENU		
	—— Close, TWE, p. 483	10–15 minutes	All levels

See Optional Resources menu on page viii.

The Way to Victory

Section 5 *(pp. 485–491)*

LOCAL OBJECTIVES	TWE—Teacher Wraparound Edition TCR—Teacher Classroom Resources 📁 Blackline Master 🎨 Transparency 💿 CD-ROM ◉ DVD 📋 Poster 🎵 Music Program 🔊 Audio Program 📼 Videocassette 🔗 Internet Resources		
	OBJECTIVES **1.** Identify the battles that turned the tide of the war in 1863. **2.** Cite the events that led to the South's surrender in 1865.		
	FOCUS MENU	**SUGGESTED TIME RANGES**	**SUGGESTED LEVEL**
	—— Daily Focus Skills Transparency 16–5, TCR 🎨 📁	5–10 minutes	L1
	—— Vocabulary PuzzleMaker CD-ROM 💿	5–10 minutes	All levels
	—— Audio Program Chapter 16 🔊	20–25 minutes	All levels
	TEACH MENU **Guided Practice**		
	—— Activity, TWE, p. 486	5–10 minutes	L1
	—— Cooperative Learning Activity, TWE, p. 486	40–60 minutes	ELL, L1
	—— Meeting Special Needs, TWE, p. 487	25–35 minutes	L1
	—— Interdisciplinary Connections Activity, TWE, p. 488	20–30 minutes	ELL, L2
	—— Critical Thinking Activity, TWE, p. 489	20–25 minutes	L2
	—— Extending the Content, TWE, p. 490	5–10 minutes	All levels
	—— Graphic Organizer Transparencies Strategies and Activities, TCR 🎨 📁	20–25 minutes	All levels
	Independent Practice		
	—— Guided Reading Activity 16–5 TCR 📁	15–20 minutes	ELL, L1
	—— Vocabulary Activity 16, TCR 📁	20–30 minutes	All levels
	—— Chapter Skills Activity 16, TCR 📁	10–15 minute	L1
	—— Critical Thinking Activity 16, TCR 📁	15–20 minutes	L1
	—— Geography and History Activity 16, TCR 📁	20–30 minutes	L1
	—— Time Line Activity 16, TCR 📁	10–15 minutes	All levels
	ASSESS MENU **Evaluate**		
	—— Section Quiz 16–5, TCR 📁	10–15 minutes	All levels
	—— Performance Assessment Activity 16, TCR 📁	25–30 minutes	All levels
	—— Interactive Tutor Self-Assessment CD-ROM 💿	20–30 minutes	All levels
	—— ExamView® Pro Testmaker CD-ROM 💿	15–20 minutes	All levels
	Reteach		
	—— Reteaching Activity 16–5, TCR 📁	15–20 minutes	ELL, L1
	—— Reading Essentials and Study Guide 16–5, TCR 📁	25–35 minutes	ELL, L1
	—— Take-Home Review Activity 16, TCR 📁	10–15 minutes	All levels
	—— MindJogger Videoquiz, Chapter 16 ◉ 📼	20–25 minutes	All levels
	Enrich		
	—— Enrichment Activity 16–5, TCR 📁	10–15 minutes	L2, L3
	CLOSE MENU		
	—— Close, TWE, p. 491	10–15 minutes	All levels

See Optional Resources menu on page viii.

Reconstruction Plans

Section 1 *(pp. 500–503)*

LOCAL OBJECTIVES	TWE—Teacher Wraparound Edition TCR—Teacher Classroom Resources
	📁 Blackline Master ▲ Transparency ⊙ CD-ROM ⊙ DVD 📕 Poster
	🎵 Music Program 🔊 Audio Program 📼 Videocassette 🖱️ Internet Resources

OBJECTIVES

1. Compare Lincoln's plan for Reconstruction and the plan of the Radical Republicans.

2. Explain Andrew Johnson's proposal for handling Reconstruction.

FOCUS MENU	SUGGESTED TIME RANGES	SUGGESTED LEVELS
—— Daily Focus Skills Transparency 17–1, TCR ▲ 📁	5–10 minutes	L1
—— Preteaching Vocabulary, TWE, p. 500	5–10 minutes	All levels
—— History Online Chapter 17 Overview 🖱️	15–20 minutes	All levels
—— Audio Program Chapter 17 🔊	20–25 minutes	All levels

TEACH MENU		
Guided Practice		
—— Time Line Activity, TWE, p. 499	10–15 minutes	All levels
—— Activity, TWE, p. 501	5–10 minutes	L2
—— Cooperative Learning Activity, TWE, p. 501	40–60 minutes	L1
—— Meeting Special Needs, TWE, p. 502	25–35 minutes	L1
—— Graphic Organizer Transparency Strategy and Activity 17, TCR ▲ 📁	15–20 minutes	L2
Independent Practice		
—— Guided Reading Activity 17–1, TCR 📁	15–20 minutes	ELL, L1
—— Reading and Study Skills Foldable, p. 499	10–15 minutes	All levels

ASSESS MENU		
Evaluate		
—— Section Quiz 17–1, TCR 📁	10–15 minutes	All levels
—— Interactive Tutor Self-Assessment CD-ROM ⊙	20–30 minutes	All levels
—— ExamView® Pro Testmaker CD-ROM ⊙	15–20 minutes	All levels
Reteach		
—— Reteaching Activity 17–1, TCR 📁	15–20 minutes	ELL, L1
—— Reading Essentials and Study Guide 17–1, TCR 📁	25–35 minutes	ELL, L1
Enrich		
—— Enrichment Activity 17–1, TCR 📁	10–15 minutes	L2, L3

CLOSE MENU		
—— Close, TWE, p. 503	10–15 minutes	All levels

See Optional Resources menu on page viii.

Grade _____ Class(es) _____ Date _____ M Tu W Th F

Teacher's Name _____ Date _____

Radicals in Control   Section 2 *(pp. 504–508)*

LOCAL OBJECTIVES	TWE—Teacher Wraparound Edition TCR—Teacher Classroom Resources 📁 Blackline Master ♨ Transparency 💿 CD-ROM 💿 DVD 📕 Poster 🎵 Music Program 🔊 Audio Program 📺 Videocassette 🖱 Internet Resources

	OBJECTIVES		
	1. Identify what some Southerners did to deprive freed people of their rights, and explain how Congress responded. **2.** Cite the main features of Radical Reconstruction.		

	FOCUS MENU	**SUGGESTED TIME RANGES**	**SUGGESTED LEVEL**
	—— Daily Focus Skills Transparency 17–2, TCR ♨ 📁	5–10 minutes	L1
	—— Preteaching Vocabulary, TWE, p. 504	5–10 minutes	All levels
	—— Audio Program Chapter 17 🔊	20–25 minutes	All levels

	TEACH MENU		
	Guided Practice		
	—— Activity, TWE, p. 505	5–10 minutes	L1
	—— Cooperative Learning Activity, TWE, p. 505	40–60 minutes	L2
	—— Meeting Special Needs, TWE, p. 506	25–35 minutes	L1
	—— Interdisciplinary Connections Activity, TWE, p. 507	20–30 minutes	L2
	—— Graphic Organizer Transparencies Strategies and Activities, TCR ♨ 📁	20–25 minutes	All levels
	Independent Practice		
	—— Guided Reading Activity 17–2, TCR 📁	15–20 minutes	ELL, L1

	ASSESS MENU		
	Evaluate		
	—— Section Quiz 17–2, TCR 📁	10–15 minutes	All levels
	—— Interactive Tutor Self-Assessment CD-ROM 💿	20–30 minutes	All levels
	—— ExamView® Pro Testmaker CD-ROM 💿	15–20 minutes	All levels
	Reteach		
	—— Reteaching Activity 17–2, TCR 📁	15–20 minutes	ELL, L1
	—— Reading Essentials and Study Guide 17–2, TCR 📁	25–35 minutes	ELL, L1
	Enrich		
	—— Enrichment Activity 17–2, TCR 📁	10–15 minutes	L2, L3
	—— Linking Past and Present Activity 17, TCR 📁	15–20 minutes	All levels

	CLOSE MENU		
	—— Close, TWE, p. 508	10–15 minutes	All levels

See Optional Resources menu on page viii.

Copyright © by The McGraw-Hill Companies, Inc.

The South During Reconstruction Section 3 *(pp. 509–512)*

LOCAL OBJECTIVES	TWE—Teacher Wraparound Edition TCR—Teacher Classroom Resources
	📁 Blackline Master ✍ Transparency 💿 CD-ROM 💿 DVD 📱 Poster
	🎵 Music Program 🎧 Audio Program 📼 Videocassette ⌁ Internet Resources

OBJECTIVES

1. Identify what groups participated in the South's Reconstruction.

2. Explain how Southern life changed during Reconstruction.

	FOCUS MENU	SUGGESTED TIME RANGES	SUGGESTED LEVEL
	____ Daily Focus Skills Transparency 17–3, TCR ✍ 📁	5–10 minutes	L1
	____ Preteaching Vocabulary, TWE, p. 509	5–10 minutes	All levels
	____ Audio Program Chapter 17 🎧	20–25 minutes	All levels

TEACH MENU

Guided Practice

	____ Activity, TWE, p. 510	5–10 minutes	L1
	____ Cooperative Learning Activity, TWE, p. 510	40–60 minutes	ELL, L1
	____ Meeting Special Needs, TWE, p. 511	25–35 minutes	L1
	____ Graphic Organizer Transparencies Strategies and Activities, TCR ✍ 📁	20–25 minutes	All levels
	____ Why It Matters Chapter Transparency Strategy and Activity 17, TCR ✍ 📁	25–30 minutes	All levels

Independent Practice

	____ Guided Reading Activity 17–3, TCR 📁	15–20 minutes	ELL, L1

ASSESS MENU

Evaluate

	____ Section Quiz 17–3, TCR 📁	10–15 minutes	All levels
	____ Interactive Tutor Self-Assessment CD-ROM 💿	20–30 minutes	All levels
	____ ExamView® Pro Testmaker CD-ROM 💿	15–20 minutes	All levels
	____ History Online Activity ⌁	15–20 minutes	All levels

Reteach

	____ Reteaching Activity 17–3, TCR 📁	15–20 minutes	ELL, L1
	____ Reading Essentials and Study Guide 17–3, TCR 📁	25–35 minutes	ELL, L1

Enrich

	____ Enrichment Activity 17–3, TCR 📁	10–15 minutes	L2, L3
	____ Primary Source Reading 17, TCR 📁	20–30 minutes	All levels

CLOSE MENU

	____ Close, TWE, p. 512	10–15 minutes	All levels

See Optional Resources menu on page viii.

Grade _____ Class(es) _____ Date _____ M Tu W Th F

Teacher's Name _____ Date _____

REPRODUCIBLE LESSON PLAN 17–4

Change in the South

Section 4 *(pp. 513–520)*

LOCAL OBJECTIVES	TWE—Teacher Wraparound Edition TCR—Teacher Classroom Resources 📁 Blackline Master ✋ Transparency 💿 CD-ROM 💿 DVD 📕 Poster 🎵 Music Program 🔊 Audio Program 📼 Videocassette 🖊 Internet Resources		
	OBJECTIVES **1.** Cite the changes that occurred in the South during the last years of Reconstruction. **2.** Describe how African Americans were denied their rights.		
	FOCUS MENU	**SUGGESTED TIME RANGES**	**SUGGESTED LEVEL**
	—— Daily Focus Skills Transparency 17–4, TCR ✋ 📁	5–10 minutes	L1
	—— Vocabulary PuzzleMaker CD-ROM 💿	5–10 minutes	All levels
	—— Audio Program Chapter 17 🔊	20–25 minutes	All levels
	TEACH MENU **Guided Practice**		
	—— Activity, TWE, p. 514	5–10 minutes	L1
	—— Cooperative Learning Activity, TWE, p. 514	40–60 minutes	ELL, L1
	—— Meeting Special Needs, TWE, p. 515	25–35 minutes	L1
	—— Interdisciplinary Connections Activity, TWE, p. 516	20–30 minutes	L3
	—— Critical Thinking Activity, TWE, p. 517	20–25 minutes	L2
	—— Extending the Content, TWE, p. 518	5–10 minutes	All levels
	—— Extending the Content, TWE, p. 519	5–10 minutes	All levels
	—— Graphic Organizer Transparencies Strategies and Activities, TCR ✋ 📁	20–25 minutes	All levels
	Independent Practice		
	—— Guided Reading Activity 17–4 TCR 📁	15–20 minutes	ELL, L1
	—— Vocabulary Activity 17, TCR 📁	20–30 minutes	All levels
	—— Chapter Skills Activity 17, TCR 📁	15–20 minutes	L1
	—— Critical Thinking Activity 17, TCR 📁	15–20 minutes	L1
	—— Geography and History Activity 17, TCR 📁	15–20 minutes	All levels
	—— Time Line Activity 17, TCR 📁	15–20 minutes	All levels
	ASSESS MENU **Evaluate**		
	—— Section Quiz 17–4, TCR 📁	10–15 minutes	All levels
	—— Performance Assessment Activity 17, TCR 📁	25–30 minutes	All levels
	—— Interactive Tutor Self-Assessment CD-ROM 💿	20–30 minutes	All levels
	—— ExamView® Pro Testmaker CD-ROM 💿	15–20 minutes	All levels
	Reteach		
	—— Reteaching Activity 17–4, TCR 📁	15–20 minutes	ELL, L1
	—— Reading Essentials and Study Guide 17–4, TCR 📁	25–35 minutes	ELL, L1
	—— Take-Home Review Activity 17, TCR 📁	10–15 minutes	All levels
	—— MindJogger Videoquiz, Chapter 17 💿 📼	20–25 minutes	All levels
	Enrich		
	—— Enrichment Activity 17–4, TCR 📁	10–15 minutes	L2, L3
	CLOSE MENU		
	—— Close, TWE, p. 520	10–15 minutes	All levels

See Optional Resources menu on page viii.

REPRODUCIBLE LESSON PLAN **18–1**

The Mining Booms — Section 1 *(pp. 528–532)*

LOCAL OBJECTIVES	TWE—Teacher Wraparound Edition TCR—Teacher Classroom Resources
	📁 Blackline Master 🖊 Transparency 💿 CD-ROM 💽 DVD 📕 Poster
	🎵 Music Program 🎧 Audio Program 📼 Videocassette 🔗 Internet Resources

	OBJECTIVES		
	1. Describe how the rush to find gold and silver led to the growth of new communities in the West.		
	2. Analyze how the development of the railroads affected the nation.		

	FOCUS MENU	**SUGGESTED TIME RANGES**	**SUGGESTED LEVELS**
	—— Daily Focus Skills Transparency 18–1, TCR 🖊 📁	5–10 minutes	L1
	—— Preteaching Vocabulary, TWE, p. 528	5–10 minutes	All levels
	—— History Online Chapter 18 Overview 🔗	15–20 minutes	All levels
	—— Audio Program Chapter 18 🎧	20–25 minutes	All levels

	TEACH MENU		
	Guided Practice		
	—— Time Line Activity, TWE, p. 527	5–10 minutes	L1
	—— Activity, TWE, p. 529	5–10 minutes	L1
	—— Cooperative Learning Activity, TWE, p. 529	40–60 minutes	ELL, L1
	—— Meeting Special Needs, TWE, p. 530	25–35 minutes	L1
	—— Interdisciplinary Connections Activity, TWE, p. 531	20–30 minutes	L2
	—— Graphic Organizer Transparencies Strategies and Activities, TCR 🖊 📁	20–25 minutes	All levels
	Independent Practice		
	—— Guided Reading Activity 18–1, TCR 📁	15–20 minutes	ELL, L1
	—— Reading and Study Skills Foldable, p. 527	10–15 minutes	All levels

	ASSESS MENU		
	Evaluate		
	—— Section Quiz 18–1, TCR 📁	10–15 minutes	All levels
	—— Interactive Tutor Self-Assessment CD-ROM 💿	20–30 minutes	All levels
	—— ExamView® Pro Testmaker CD-ROM 💿	15–20 minutes	All levels
	Reteach		
	—— Reteaching Activity 18–1, TCR 📁	15–20 minutes	ELL, L1
	—— Reading Essentials and Study Guide 18–1, TCR 📁	25–35 minutes	ELL, L1
	Enrich		
	—— Enrichment Activity 18–1, TCR 📁	10–15 minutes	L2, L3
	—— Primary Source Reading 18, TCR 📁	20–30 minutes	All levels

	CLOSE MENU		
	—— Close, TWE, p. 532	10–15 minutes	All levels

See Optional Resources menu on page viii.

Ranchers and Farmers

Section 2 *(pp. 534–539)*

LOCAL OBJECTIVES	TWE—Teacher Wraparound Edition TCR—Teacher Classroom Resources 📁 Blackline Master 🔲 Transparency 🔘 CD-ROM 🔘 DVD 🗒 Poster 🎵 Music Program 🔊 Audio Program 📼 Videocassette ✒ Internet Resources		
	OBJECTIVES **1.** Explain how the railroads helped create a "Cattle Kingdom" in the Southwest. **2.** Discuss how women contributed to the settling of the Great Plains.		
	FOCUS MENU	**SUGGESTED TIME RANGES**	**SUGGESTED LEVELS**
	____ Daily Focus Skills Transparency 18–2, TCR 🔲 📁	5–10 minutes	L1
	____ Preteaching Vocabulary, TWE, p. 534	5–10 minutes	All levels
	____ Audio Program Chapter 18 🔊	20–25 minutes	All levels
	TEACH MENU **Guided Practice**		
	____ Activity, TWE, p. 535	5–10 minutes	L1
	____ Cooperative Learning Activity, TWE, p. 535	40–60 minutes	ELL, L1
	____ Meeting Special Needs, TWE, p. 536	25–35 minutes	L1
	____ Interdisciplinary Connections Activity, TWE, p. 537	20–30 minutes	L2
	____ Critical Thinking Activity, TWE, p. 538	20–25 minutes	L1
	____ Graphic Organizer Transparency Strategy and Activity 18, TCR 🔲 📁	15–20 minutes	L2
	____ Why It Matters Chapter Transparency Strategy and Activity 18, TCR 🔲 📁	25–30 minutes	All levels
	Independent Practice		
	____ Guided Reading Activity 18–2, TCR 📁	15–20 minutes	ELL, L1
	ASSESS MENU **Evaluate**		
	____ Section Quiz 18–2, TCR 📁	10–15 minutes	All levels
	____ Interactive Tutor Self-Assessment CD-ROM 🔘	20–30 minutes	All levels
	____ ExamView® Pro Testmaker CD-ROM 🔘	15–20 minutes	All levels
	Reteach		
	____ Reteaching Activity 18–2, TCR 📁	15–20 minutes	ELL, L1
	____ Reading Essentials and Study Guide 18–2, TCR 📁	25–35 minutes	ELL, L1
	Enrich		
	____ Enrichment Activity 18–2, TCR 📁	10–15 minutes	L2, L3
	____ Linking Past and Present Activity 18, TCR 📁	15–20 minutes	All levels
	CLOSE MENU		
	____ Close, TWE, p. 539	10–15 minutes	All levels

See Optional Resources menu on page viii.

Native American Struggles   Section 3 *(pp. 542–547)*

LOCAL OBJECTIVES	TWE—Teacher Wraparound Edition TCR—Teacher Classroom Resources
	🗁 Blackline Master 🎙 Transparency 💿 CD-ROM 💿 DVD 📕 Poster
	🎵 Music Program 🎧 Audio Program 📼 Videocassette 🔌 Internet Resources

	OBJECTIVES
	1. Explain why the federal government forced Native Americans to move to reservations.
	2. Describe how conflict between Native Americans and whites grew.

	FOCUS MENU	**SUGGESTED TIME RANGES**	**SUGGESTED LEVELS**
	—— Daily Focus Skills Transparency 18–3, TCR 🎙 🗁	5–10 minutes	L1
	—— Preteaching Vocabulary, TWE, p. 542	5–10 minutes	All levels
	—— Audio Program Chapter 18 🎧	20–25 minutes	All levels

	TEACH MENU		
	Guided Practice		
	—— Activity, TWE, p. 543	5–10 minutes	L1
	—— Cooperative Learning Activity, TWE, p. 543	40–60 minutes	ELL, L1
	—— Meeting Special Needs, TWE, p. 544	25–35 minutes	L1
	—— Interdisciplinary Connections Activity, TWE, p. 545	20–30 minutes	L2
	—— Critical Thinking Activity, TWE, p. 546	20–30 minutes	L1
	—— Graphic Organizer Transparencies Strategies and Activities, TCR 🎙 🗁	20–25 minutes	All levels
	Independent Practice		
	—— Guided Reading Activity 18–3, TCR 🗁	15–20 minutes	ELL, L1

	ASSESS MENU		
	Evaluate		
	—— Section Quiz 18–3, TCR 🗁	10–15 minutes	All levels
	—— Interactive Tutor Self-Assessment CD-ROM 💿	20–30 minutes	All levels
	—— ExamView® Pro Testmaker CD-ROM 💿	15–20 minutes	All levels
	Reteach		
	—— Reteaching Activity 18–3, TCR 🗁	15–20 minutes	ELL, L1
	—— Reading Essentials and Study Guide 18–3, TCR 🗁	25–35 minutes	ELL, L1
	Enrich		
	—— Enrichment Activity 18–3, TCR 🗁	10–15 minutes	L2, L3

	CLOSE MENU		
	—— Close, TWE, p. 547	10–15 minutes	All levels

See Optional Resources menu on page viii.

Farmers in Protest

Section 4 *(pp. 548–551)*

LOCAL OBJECTIVES	TWE—Teacher Wraparound Edition TCR—Teacher Classroom Resources 📁 Blackline Master 🖋 Transparency 💿 CD-ROM 💿 DVD 📙 Poster 🎵 Music Program 🎧 Audio Program 📼 Videocassette 🔌 Internet Resources		
	OBJECTIVES **1.** Summarize why farmers faced hard times in the late 1800s. **2.** Explain how farmers tried to solve their problems.		
	FOCUS MENU	**SUGGESTED TIME RANGES**	**SUGGESTED LEVELS**
	—— Daily Focus Skills Transparency 18–4, TCR 🖋 📁	5–10 minutes	L1
	—— Vocabulary PuzzleMaker CD-ROM 💿	5–10 minutes	All levels
	—— Audio Program Chapter 18 🎧	20–25 minutes	All levels
	TEACH MENU **Guided Practice**		
	—— Activity, TWE, p. 549	5–10 minutes	L1
	—— Cooperative Learning Activity, TWE, p. 549	40–60 minutes	L2
	—— Meeting Special Needs, TWE, p. 550	25–35 minutes	L1
	—— Graphic Organizer Transparencies Strategies and Activities, TCR 🖋 📁	20–25 minutes	All levels
	Independent Practice		
	—— Guided Reading Activity 18–4 TCR 📁	15–20 minutes	ELL, L1
	—— Vocabulary Activity 18, TCR 📁	20–30 minutes	All levels
	—— Chapter Skills Activity 18, TCR 📁	10–15 minutes	L1
	—— Critical Thinking Activity 18, TCR 📁	15–20 minutes	L2, L3
	—— Geography and History Activity 18, TCR 📁	10–15 minutes	All levels
	—— Time Line Activity 18, TCR 📁	10–15 minutes	All levels
	ASSESS MENU **Evaluate**		
	—— Section Quiz 18–4, TCR 📁	10–15 minutes	All levels
	—— Performance Assessment Activity 18, TCR 📁	25–30 minutes	All levels
	—— Interactive Tutor Self-Assessment CD-ROM 💿	20–30 minutes	All levels
	—— ExamView® Pro Testmaker CD-ROM 💿	15–20 minutes	All levels
	—— History Online Activity 🔌	15–20 minutes	All levels
	Reteach		
	—— Reteaching Activity 18–4, TCR 📁	15–20 minutes	ELL, L1
	—— Reading Essentials and Study Guide 18–4, TCR 📁	25–35 minutes	ELL, L1
	—— Take-Home Review Activity 18, TCR 📁	10–15 minutes	All levels
	—— MindJogger Videoquiz, Chapter 18 💿 📼	20–25 minutes	All levels
	Enrich		
	—— Enrichment Activity 18–4, TCR 📁	10–15 minutes	L2, L3
	CLOSE MENU —— Close, TWE, p. 551	10–15 minutes	All levels

See Optional Resources menu on page viii.

Railroads Lead the Way
Section 1 (pp. 556–559)

LOCAL OBJECTIVES	TWE—Teacher Wraparound Edition · · · · · · · · · · · · · · · · · · TCR—Teacher Classroom Resources
	📁 Blackline Master · · 🖐 Transparency · · 💿 CD-ROM · · 📀 DVD · · 📗 Poster
	🎵 Music Program · · 🔊 Audio Program · · 📼 Videocassette · · 🌐 Internet Resources

	OBJECTIVES **1.** Explain how the railroad barons made huge fortunes. **2.** Understand how the national railroad system changed the American economy.

		SUGGESTED TIME RANGES	SUGGESTED LEVELS
	FOCUS MENU		
	—— Daily Focus Skills Transparency 19–1, TCR 🖐 📁	5–10 minutes	L1
	—— Preteaching Vocabulary, TWE, p. 556	5–10 minutes	All levels
	—— History Online Chapter 19 Overview 🌐	15–20 minutes	All levels
	—— Audio Program Chapter 19 🔊	20–25 minutes	All levels
	TEACH MENU **Guided Practice**		
	—— Time Line Activity, TWE, p. 555	5–10 minutes	L1
	—— Activity, TWE, p. 557	5–10 minutes	L1
	—— Cooperative Learning Activity, TWE, p. 557	40–60 minutes	L2
	—— Meeting Special Needs, TWE, p. 558	25–35 minutes	L1
	—— Graphic Organizer Transparencies Strategies and Activities, TCR 🖐 📁	20–25 minutes	All levels
	Independent Practice		
	—— Guided Reading Activity 19–1, TCR 📁	15–20 minutes	ELL, L1
	—— Reading and Study Skills Foldable, p. 555	10–15 minutes	All levels
	ASSESS MENU **Evaluate**		
	—— Section Quiz 19–1, TCR 📁	10–15 minutes	All levels
	—— Interactive Tutor Self-Assessment CD-ROM 💿	20–30 minutes	All levels
	—— ExamView® Pro Testmaker CD-ROM 💿	15–20 minutes	All levels
	Reteach		
	—— Reteaching Activity 19–1, TCR 📁	15–20 minutes	ELL, L1
	—— Reading Essentials and Study Guide 19–1, TCR 📁	25–35 minutes	ELL, L1
	Enrich		
	—— Enrichment Activity 19–1, TCR 📁	10–15 minutes	L2, L3
	CLOSE MENU		
	—— Close, TWE, p. 559	10–15 minutes	All levels

See Optional Resources menu on page viii.

Grade _____   Class(es) _____   Date _____   M Tu W Th F

Teacher's Name _____   Date _____

Inventions

Section 2 *(pp. 561–566)*

LOCAL OBJECTIVES	TWE—Teacher Wraparound Edition TCR—Teacher Classroom Resources 📁 Blackline Master ✋ Transparency 💿 CD-ROM 💿 DVD 📱 Poster 🎵 Music Program 🔊 Audio Program 📼 Videocassette 🖇 Internet Resources

	OBJECTIVES 1. Identify what changes in transportation and communication transformed America. 2. Summarize how labor-saving inventions affected life.		

	FOCUS MENU	**SUGGESTED TIME RANGES**	**SUGGESTED LEVELS**
	—— Daily Focus Skills Transparency 19–2, TCR ✋ 📁	5–10 minutes	L1
	—— Preteaching Vocabulary, TWE, p. 561	5–10 minutes	All levels
	—— Audio Program Chapter 19 🔊	20–25 minutes	All levels

	TEACH MENU **Guided Practice**		
	—— Activity, TWE, p. 562	5–10 minutes	L1
	—— Cooperative Learning Activity, TWE, p. 562	40–60 minutes	L1
	—— Meeting Special Needs, TWE, p. 563	25–35 minutes	L1
	—— Interdisciplinary Connections Activity, TWE, p. 564	20–30 minutes	ELL, L2
	—— Critical Thinking Activity, TWE, p. 565	20–25 minutes	L3
	—— Graphic Organizer Transparencies Strategies and Activities, TCR ✋ 📁	20–25 minutes	All levels
	—— Why It Matters Chapter Transparency Strategy and Activity 19, TCR ✋ 📁	25–30 minutes	All levels
	Independent Practice		
	—— Guided Reading Activity 19–2, TCR 📁	15–20 minutes	ELL, L1

	ASSESS MENU **Evaluate**		
	—— Section Quiz 19–2, TCR 📁	10–15 minutes	All levels
	—— Interactive Tutor Self-Assessment CD-ROM 💿	20–30 minutes	All levels
	—— ExamView® Pro Testmaker CD-ROM 💿	15–20 minutes	All levels
	—— History Online Activity 🖇	15–20 minutes	All levels
	Reteach		
	—— Reteaching Activity 19–2, TCR 📁	15–20 minutes	ELL, L1
	—— Reading Essentials and Study Guide 19–2, TCR 📁	25–35 minutes	ELL, L1
	Enrich		
	—— Enrichment Activity 19–2, TCR 📁	10–15 minutes	L2, L3
	—— Linking Past and Present Activity 19, TCR 📁	15–20 minutes	All levels

	CLOSE MENU		
	—— Close, TWE, p. 566	10–15 minutes	All levels

See Optional Resources menu on page viii.

The American Journey

An Age of Big Business   Section 3 *(pp. 567–571)*

LOCAL OBJECTIVES	TWE—Teacher Wraparound Edition TCR—Teacher Classroom Resources 📁 Blackline Master 🖎 Transparency 📀 CD-ROM ⊚ DVD 📱 Poster 🎵 Music Program 🔊 Audio Program 📼 Videocassette ⬤⟋ Internet Resources

	OBJECTIVES **1.** Explain how new discoveries and inventions helped industries grow. **2.** Explore why the development of large corporations brought both benefits and problems.		

	FOCUS MENU	**SUGGESTED TIME RANGES**	**SUGGESTED LEVELS**
	—— Daily Focus Skills Transparency 19–3, TCR 🖎 📁	5–10 minutes	L1
	—— Preteaching Vocabulary, TWE, p. 567	5–10 minutes	All levels
	—— Audio Program Chapter 19 🔊	20–25 minutes	All levels

	TEACH MENU		
	Guided Practice		
	—— Activity, TWE, p. 568	5–10 minutes	L1
	—— Cooperative Learning Activity, TWE, p. 568	40–60 minutes	L2
	—— Meeting Special Needs, TWE, p. 569	25–35 minutes	L1
	—— Interdisciplinary Connections Activity, TWE, p. 570	20–30 minutes	ELL, L2
	—— Graphic Organizer Transparencies Strategies and Activities, TCR 🖎 📁	20–25 minutes	All levels
	—— American Art and Architecture 🖎 📁	20–30 minutes	All levels
	Independent Practice		
	—— Guided Reading Activity 19–3, TCR 📁	15–20 minutes	ELL, L1

	ASSESS MENU		
	Evaluate		
	—— Section Quiz 19–3, TCR 📁	10–15 minutes	All levels
	—— Interactive Tutor Self-Assessment CD-ROM 📀	20–30 minutes	All levels
	—— ExamView® Pro Testmaker CD-ROM 📀	15–20 minutes	All levels
	Reteach		
	—— Reteaching Activity 19–3, TCR 📁	15–20 minutes	ELL, L1
	—— Reading Essentials and Study Guide 19–3, TCR 📁	25–35 minutes	ELL, L1
	Enrich		
	—— Enrichment Activity 19–3, TCR 📁	10–15 minutes	L2, L3
	—— Primary Source Reading 19, TCR 📁	20–30 minutes	All levels

	CLOSE MENU		
	—— Close, TWE, p. 571	10–15 minutes	All levels

See Optional Resources menu on page viii.

Industrial Workers

Section 4 *(pp. 572–575)*

LOCAL OBJECTIVES	TWE—Teacher Wraparound Edition TCR—Teacher Classroom Resources 📁 Blackline Master ✋ Transparency 💿 CD-ROM 💿 DVD 📄 Poster 🎵 Music Program 🎧 Audio Program 📼 Videocassette 🖱 Internet Resources		
	OBJECTIVES **1.** Explain why workers demanded changes in their working conditions and wages. **2.** Identify how labor unions helped workers gain economic and political power.		
	FOCUS MENU	**SUGGESTED TIME RANGES**	**SUGGESTED LEVELS**
	—— Daily Focus Skills Transparency 19–4, TCR ✋ 📁	5–10 minutes	L1
	—— Vocabulary PuzzleMaker CD-ROM 💿	5–10 minutes	All levels
	—— Audio Program Chapter 19 🎧	20–25 minutes	All levels
	TEACH MENU **Guided Practice**		
	—— Activity, TWE, p. 573	5–10 minutes	L1
	—— Cooperative Learning Activity, TWE, p. 573	40–60 minutes	ELL, L2
	—— Meeting Special Needs, TWE, p. 574	25–35 minutes	L1
	—— Graphic Organizer Transparency Strategy and Activity 19, TCR ✋ 📁	15–20 minutes	L2
	Independent Practice		
	—— Guided Reading Activity 19–4 TCR 📁	15–20 minutes	ELL, L1
	—— Vocabulary Activity 19, TCR 📁	20–30 minutes	All levels
	—— Chapter Skills Activity 19, TCR 📁	10–15 minutes	L1
	—— Critical Thinking Activity 19, TCR 📁	10–15 minutes	L1
	—— Geography and History Activity 19, TCR 📁	15–20 minutes	All levels
	—— Time Line Activity 19, TCR 📁	10–15 minutes	All levels
	ASSESS MENU **Evaluate**		
	—— Section Quiz 19–4, TCR 📁	10–15 minutes	All levels
	—— Performance Assessment Activity 19, TCR 📁	25–30 minutes	All levels
	—— Interactive Tutor Self-Assessment CD-ROM 💿	20–30 minutes	All levels
	—— ExamView® Pro Testmaker CD-ROM 💿	15–20 minutes	All levels
	Reteach		
	—— Reteaching Activity 19–4, TCR 📁	15–20 minutes	ELL, L1
	—— Reading Essentials and Study Guide 19–4, TCR 📁	25–35 minutes	ELL, L1
	—— Take-Home Review Activity 19, TCR 📁	10–15 minutes	All levels
	—— MindJogger Videoquiz, Chapter 19 💿 📼	20–25 minutes	All levels
	Enrich		
	—— Enrichment Activity 19–4, TCR 📁	10–15 minutes	L2, L3
	CLOSE MENU —— Close, TWE, p. 575	10–15 minutes	All levels

See Optional Resources menu on page viii.

The New Immigrants

Section 1 (pp. 582–587)

LOCAL OBJECTIVES	TWE—Teacher Wraparound Edition TCR—Teacher Classroom Resources 🗀 Blackline Master 🖋 Transparency ◉ CD-ROM ◉ DVD 📕 Poster 🎵 Music Program ◉ Audio Program 📼 Videocassette ➹ Internet Resources

	OBJECTIVES **1.** Explore what opportunities and difficulties immigrants found in the United States. **2.** Understand how the arrival of new immigrants changed American Society.		

	FOCUS MENU	**SUGGESTED TIME RANGES**	**SUGGESTED LEVELS**
	—— Daily Focus Skills Transparency 20–1, TCR 🖋 🗀	5–10 minutes	L1
	—— Preteaching Vocabulary, TWE, p. 582	5–10 minutes	All levels
	—— History Online Chapter 20 Overview ➹	15–20 minutes	All levels
	—— Audio Program Chapter 20 ◉	20–25 minutes	All levels

	TEACH MENU		
	Guided Practice		
	—— Time Line Activity, TWE, p. 581	10–15 minutes	L1
	—— Activity, TWE, p. 583	5–10 minutes	L1
	—— Cooperative Learning Activity, TWE, p. 583	40–60 minutes	L2
	—— Meeting Special Needs, TWE, p. 584	25–35 minutes	L1
	—— Interdisciplinary Connections Activity, TWE, p. 585	20–30 minutes	ELL, L1
	—— Critical Thinking Activity, TWE, p. 586	20–25 minutes	L3
	—— Graphic Organizer Transparencies Strategies and Activities, TCR 🖋 🗀	20–25 minutes	All levels
	Independent Practice		
	—— Guided Reading Activity 20–1, TCR 🗀	15–20 minutes	ELL, L1
	—— Reading and Study Skills Foldable, p. 581	10–15 minutes	All levels

	ASSESS MENU		
	Evaluate		
	—— Section Quiz 20–1, TCR 🗀	10–15 minutes	All levels
	—— Interactive Tutor Self-Assessment CD-ROM ◉	20–30 minutes	All levels
	—— ExamView® Pro Testmaker CD-ROM ◉	15–20 minutes	All levels
	—— History Online Activity ➹	15–20 minutes	All levels
	Reteach		
	—— Reteaching Activity 20–1, TCR 🗀	15–20 minutes	ELL, L1
	—— Reading Essentials and Study Guide 20–1, TCR 🗀	25–35 minutes	ELL, L1
	Enrich		
	—— Enrichment Activity 20–1, TCR 🗀	10–15 minutes	L2, L3

	CLOSE MENU		
	—— Close, TWE, p. 587	10–15 minutes	All levels

See Optional Resources menu on page viii.

Grade _____ Class(es) _____ Date _____ M Tu W Th F

Teacher's Name _____ Date _____

Moving to the City
Section 2 (pp. 590–595)

LOCAL OBJECTIVES	TWE—Teacher Wraparound Edition TCR—Teacher Classroom Resources
	📁 Blackline Master 🔖 Transparency 💿 CD-ROM 💿 DVD 📕 Poster
	🎵 Music Program 🎧 Audio Program 📼 Videocassette 🖱 Internet Resources

	OBJECTIVES		
	1. Explain how American cities grew and changed.		
	2. Summarize what problems cities faced and how people tried to solve them.		

	FOCUS MENU	**SUGGESTED TIME RANGES**	**SUGGESTED LEVELS**
	—— Daily Focus Skills Transparency 20–2, TCR 🔖 📁	5–10 minutes	L1
	—— Preteaching Vocabulary, TWE, p. 590	5–10 minutes	All levels
	—— Audio Program Chapter 20 🎧	20–25 minutes	All levels

	TEACH MENU		
	Guided Practice		
	—— Activity, TWE, p. 591	5–10 minutes	ELL, L1
	—— Cooperative Learning Activity, TWE, p. 591	40–60 minutes	L2
	—— Meeting Special Needs, TWE, p. 592	25–35 minutes	L1
	—— Interdisciplinary Connections Activity, TWE, p. 593	20–30 minutes	L3
	—— Critical Thinking Activity, TWE, p. 594	20–25 minutes	L2
	—— Graphic Organizer Transparency Strategy and Activity 20, TCR 🔖 📁	15–20 minutes	L2
	—— Why It Matters Chapter Transparency Strategy and Activity 20, TCR 🔖 📁	25–30 minutes	All levels
	Independent Practice		
	—— Guided Reading Activity 20–2, TCR 📁	15–20 minutes	ELL, L1

	ASSESS MENU		
	Evaluate		
	—— Section Quiz 20–2, TCR 📁	10–15 minutes	All levels
	—— Interactive Tutor Self-Assessment CD-ROM 💿	20–30 minutes	All levels
	—— ExamView® Pro Testmaker CD-ROM 💿	15–20 minutes	All levels
	Reteach		
	—— Reteaching Activity 20–2, TCR 📁	15–20 minutes	ELL, L1
	—— Reading Essentials and Study Guide 20–2, TCR 📁	25–35 minutes	ELL, L1
	Enrich		
	—— Enrichment Activity 20–2, TCR 📁	10–15 minutes	L2, L3
	—— Linking Past and Present Activity 20, TCR 📁	15–20 minutes	All levels

	CLOSE MENU		
	—— Close, TWE, p. 595	10–15 minutes	All levels

See Optional Resources menu on page viii.

A Changing Culture
Section 3 (pp. 597–602)

LOCAL OBJECTIVES	TWE—Teacher Wraparound Edition TCR—Teacher Classroom Resources
	📁 Blackline Master 🗜 Transparency 💿 CD-ROM 💽 DVD 📙 Poster
	🎵 Music Program 🎧 Audio Program 📼 Videocassette ⬤◞ Internet Resources

	OBJECTIVES
	1. Explain how education became more widely available.
	2. Investigate how Americans spent their leisure time.

	FOCUS MENU	SUGGESTED TIME RANGES	SUGGESTED LEVELS
	—— Daily Focus Skills Transparency 20–3, TCR 🗜 📁	5–10 minutes	L1
	—— Vocabulary PuzzleMaker CD-ROM 💿	5–10 minutes	All levels
	—— Audio Program Chapter 20 🎧	20–25 minutes	All levels

	TEACH MENU		
	Guided Practice		
	—— Activity, TWE, p. 598	5–10 minutes	L1
	—— Cooperative Learning Activity, TWE, p. 598	40–60 minutes	L2
	—— Meeting Special Needs, TWE, p. 599	25–35 minutes	L1
	—— Interdisciplinary Connections Activity, TWE, p. 600	20–30 minutes	L1
	—— Critical Thinking Activity, TWE, p. 601	20–25 minutes	L2
	—— Graphic Organizer Transparencies Strategies and Activities, TCR 🗜 📁	20–25 minutes	All levels
	—— American Art and Architecture 🗜 📁	20–30 minutes	All levels
	Independent Practice		
	—— Guided Reading Activity 20–3, TCR 📁	15–20 minutes	ELL, L1
	—— Vocabulary Activity 20, TCR 📁	20–30 minutes	All levels
	—— Chapter Skills Activity 20, TCR 📁	20–30 minutes	All levels
	—— Critical Thinking Activity 20, TCR 📁	15–20 minutes	L1
	—— Geography and History Activity 20, TCR 📁	10–15 minutes	All levels
	—— Time Line Activity 20, TCR 📁	15–20 minutes	All levels

	ASSESS MENU		
	Evaluate		
	—— Section Quiz 20–3, TCR 📁	10–15 minutes	All levels
	—— Performance Assessment Activity 20, TCR 📁	25–30 minutes	All levels
	—— Interactive Tutor Self-Assessment CD-ROM 💿	20–30 minutes	All levels
	—— ExamView® Pro Testmaker CD-ROM 💿	15–20 minutes	All levels
	Reteach		
	—— Reteaching Activity 20–3, TCR 📁	15–20 minutes	ELL, L1
	—— Reading Essentials and Study Guide 20–3, TCR 📁	25–35 minutes	ELL, L1
	—— Take-Home Review Activity 20, TCR 📁	10–15 minutes	All levels
	—— MindJogger Videoquiz, Chapter 20 💽 📼	20–25 minutes	All levels
	Enrich		
	—— Enrichment Activity 20–3, TCR 📁	10–15 minutes	L2, L3
	—— Primary Source Reading 20, TCR 📁	20–30 minutes	All levels

	CLOSE MENU		
	—— Close, TWE, p. 602	10–15 minutes	All levels

See Optional Resources menu on page viii.

The Progressive Movement   Section 1 *(pp. 610–614)*

LOCAL OBJECTIVES	TWE—Teacher Wraparound Edition TCR—Teacher Classroom Resources Blackline Master Transparency CD-ROM DVD Poster Music Program Audio Program Videocassette Internet Resources
	OBJECTIVES **1.** Explain how journalists helped shape the reform movement. **2.** Discuss how cities, states, and Congress answered the call for reform of the government.

		SUGGESTED TIME RANGES	SUGGESTED LEVELS
	FOCUS MENU		
	—— Daily Focus Skills Transparency 21–1, TCR	5–10 minutes	L1
	—— Preteaching Vocabulary, TWE, p. 610	5–10 minutes	All levels
	—— History Online Chapter 21 Overview	15–20 minutes	All levels
	—— Audio Program Chapter 21	20–25 minutes	All levels
	TEACH MENU		
	Guided Practice		
	—— Time Line Activity, TWE, p. 609	10–15 minutes	All levels
	—— Activity, TWE, p. 611	5–10 minutes	ELL, L1
	—— Cooperative Learning Activity, TWE, p. 611	40–60 minutes	L1
	—— Meeting Special Needs, TWE, p. 612	25–35 minutes	L1
	—— Interdisciplinary Connections Activity, TWE, p. 613	20–30 minutes	L2
	—— Graphic Organizer Transparencies Strategies and Activities, TCR	20–25 minutes	All levels
	Independent Practice		
	—— Guided Reading Activity 21–1, TCR	15–20 minutes	ELL, L1
	—— Reading and Study Skills Foldable, p. 609	10–15 minutes	All levels
	ASSESS MENU		
	Evaluate		
	—— Section Quiz 21–1, TCR	10–15 minutes	All levels
	—— Interactive Tutor Self-Assessment CD-ROM	20–30 minutes	All levels
	—— ExamView® Pro Testmaker CD-ROM	15–20 minutes	All levels
	—— History Online Activity	15–20 minutes	All levels
	Reteach		
	—— Reteaching Activity 21–1, TCR	15–20 minutes	ELL, L1
	—— Reading Essentials and Study Guide 21–1, TCR	25–35 minutes	ELL, L1
	Enrich		
	—— Enrichment Activity 21–1, TCR	10–15 minutes	L2, L3
	CLOSE MENU		
	—— Close, TWE, p. 614	10–15 minutes	All levels

See Optional Resources menu on page viii.

Women and Progressives Section 2 (*pp. 615–619*)

LOCAL OBJECTIVES	TWE—Teacher Wraparound Edition TCR—Teacher Classroom Resources
	📁 Blackline Master 📓 Transparency 💿 CD-ROM ⊙ DVD 📕 Poster
	🎵 Music Program 🎧 Audio Program 📼 Videocassette 🔗 Internet Resources

OBJECTIVES

1. Describe how the role of women in American society changed during the Progressive Era.

2. Identify the ways in which women fought for the right to vote.

FOCUS MENU	SUGGESTED TIME RANGES	SUGGESTED LEVELS
—— Daily Focus Skills Transparency 21–2, TCR 📓 📁	5–10 minutes	L1
—— Preteaching Vocabulary, TWE, p. 615	5–10 minutes	All levels
—— Audio Program Chapter 21 🎧	20–25 minutes	All levels

TEACH MENU

Guided Practice

—— Activity, TWE, p. 616	5–10 minutes	L1
—— Cooperative Learning Activity, TWE, p. 616	40–60 minutes	L2
—— Meeting Special Needs, TWE, p. 617	25–35 minutes	L1
—— Interdisciplinary Connections Activity, TWE, p. 618	20–30 minutes	L3
—— Graphic Organizer Transparencies Strategies and Activities, TCR 📓 📁	20–25 minutes	All levels
—— Why It Matters Chapter Transparency Strategy and Activity 21, TCR 📓 📁	25–30 minutes	All levels

Independent Practice

—— Guided Reading Activity 21–2, TCR 📁	15–20 minutes	ELL, L1

ASSESS MENU

Evaluate

—— Section Quiz 21–2, TCR 📁	10–15 minutes	All levels
—— Interactive Tutor Self-Assessment CD-ROM 💿	20–30 minutes	All levels
—— ExamView® Pro Testmaker CD-ROM 💿	15–20 minutes	All levels

Reteach

—— Reteaching Activity 21–2, TCR 📁	15–20 minutes	ELL, L1
—— Reading Essentials and Study Guide 21–2, TCR 📁	25–35 minutes	ELL, L1

Enrich

—— Enrichment Activity 21–2, TCR 📁	10–15 minutes	L2, L3
—— Primary Source Reading 21, TCR 📁	20–30 minutes	All levels

CLOSE MENU

—— Close, TWE, p. 619	10–15 minutes	All levels

See Optional Resources menu on page viii.

Grade _____   Class(es) _____   Date _____   M Tu W Th F

Teacher's Name _____   Date _____

Progressive Presidents   Section 3 *(pp. 620–624)*

LOCAL OBJECTIVES	TWE—Teacher Wraparound Edition TCR—Teacher Classroom Resources 📁 Blackline Master 📠 Transparency 💿 CD-ROM 💿 DVD 📙 Poster 🎵 Music Program 🎧 Audio Program 📼 Videocassette 🔗 Internet Resources

	OBJECTIVES		
	1. Discuss how President Theodore Roosevelt took on big business.		
	2. Understand why the Progressives formed their own political party.		

	FOCUS MENU	**SUGGESTED TIME RANGES**	**SUGGESTED LEVELS**
	—— Daily Focus Skills Transparency 21–3, TCR 📠 📁	5–10 minutes	L1
	—— Preteaching Vocabulary, TWE, p. 620	5–10 minutes	All levels
	—— Audio Program Chapter 21 🎧	20–25 minutes	All levels

	TEACH MENU		
	Guided Practice		
	—— Activity, TWE, p. 621	5–10 minutes	ELL, L1
	—— Cooperative Learning Activity, TWE, p. 621	40–60 minutes	L3
	—— Meeting Special Needs, TWE, p. 622	25–35 minutes	L1
	—— Interdisciplinary Connections Activity, TWE, p. 623	20–30 minutes	L2
	—— Graphic Organizer Transparency Strategy and Activity 21, TCR 📠 📁	15–20 minutes	L2
	Independent Practice		
	—— Guided Reading Activity 21–3, TCR 📁	15–20 minutes	ELL, L1

	ASSESS MENU		
	Evaluate		
	—— Section Quiz 21–3, TCR 📁	10–15 minutes	All levels
	—— Interactive Tutor Self-Assessment CD-ROM 💿	20–30 minutes	All levels
	—— ExamView® Pro Testmaker CD-ROM 💿	15–20 minutes	All levels
	Reteach		
	—— Reteaching Activity 21–3, TCR 📁	15–20 minutes	ELL, L1
	—— Reading Essentials and Study Guide 21–3, TCR 📁	25–35 minutes	ELL, L1
	Enrich		
	—— Enrichment Activity 21–3, TCR 📁	10–15 minutes	L2, L3
	—— Linking Past and Present Activity 21, TCR 📁	15–20 minutes	All levels

	CLOSE MENU		
	—— Close, TWE, p. 624	10–15 minutes	All levels

See Optional Resources menu on page viii.

REPRODUCIBLE LESSON PLAN 21–4

Excluded from Reform

Section 4 (pp. 628–633)

LOCAL OBJECTIVES	TWE—Teacher Wraparound Edition TCR—Teacher Classroom Resources
	📁 Blackline Master ✍ Transparency 💿 CD-ROM 💿 DVD 📱 Poster
	🏁 Music Program 🎧 Audio Program 📼 Videocassette 🔗 Internet Resources

	OBJECTIVES **1.** Explain why progressive reforms did not include all Americans. **2.** Review how minorities worked to move toward greater equality.		
	FOCUS MENU	**SUGGESTED TIME RANGES**	**SUGGESTED LEVELS**
	____ Daily Focus Skills Transparency 21–4, TCR ✍ 📁	5–10 minutes	L1
	____ Vocabulary PuzzleMaker CD-ROM 💿	5–10 minutes	All levels
	____ Audio Program Chapter 21 🎧	20–25 minutes	All levels
	TEACH MENU **Guided Practice**		
	____ Activity, TWE, p. 629	5–10 minutes	ELL, L1
	____ Cooperative Learning Activity, TWE, p. 629	40–60 minutes	L2
	____ Meeting Special Needs, TWE, p. 630	25–35 minutes	L3
	____ Interdisciplinary Connections Activity, TWE, p. 631	20–30 minutes	L2
	____ Critical Thinking Activity, TWE, p. 632	20–25 minutes	L2
	____ Graphic Organizer Transparencies Strategies and Activities, TCR ✍ 📁	20–25 minutes	All levels
	Independent Practice		
	____ Guided Reading Activity 21–4 TCR 📁	15–20 minutes	ELL, L1
	____ Vocabulary Activity 21, TCR 📁	20–30 minutes	All levels
	____ Chapter Skills Activity 21, TCR 📁	40–60 minutes	L2, L3
	____ Critical Thinking Activity 21, TCR 📁	20–30 minutes	All levels
	____ Geography and History Activity 21, TCR 📁	20–30 minutes	L1
	____ Time Line Activity 21, TCR 📁	10–15 minutes	All levels
	ASSESS MENU **Evaluate**		
	____ Section Quiz 21–4, TCR 📁	10–15 minutes	All levels
	____ Performance Assessment Activity 21, TCR 📁	25–30 minutes	All levels
	____ Interactive Tutor Self-Assessment CD-ROM 💿	20–30 minutes	All levels
	____ ExamView® Pro Testmaker CD-ROM 💿	15–20 minutes	All levels
	Reteach		
	____ Reteaching Activity 21–4, TCR 📁	15–20 minutes	ELL, L1
	____ Reading Essentials and Study Guide 21–4, TCR 📁	25–35 minutes	ELL, L1
	____ Take-Home Review Activity 21, TCR 📁	10–15 minutes	All levels
	____ MindJogger Videoquiz, Chapter 21 💿 📼	20–25 minutes	All levels
	Enrich		
	____ Enrichment Activity 21–4, TCR 📁	10–15 minutes	L2, L3
	CLOSE MENU ____ Close, TWE, p. 633	10–15 minutes	All levels

See Optional Resources menu on page viii.

Expanding Horizons

Section 1 (pp. 638–641)

LOCAL OBJECTIVES	TWE—Teacher Wraparound Edition TCR—Teacher Classroom Resources 📁 Blackline Master 🖋 Transparency 💿 CD-ROM ◉ DVD 📕 Poster 📖 Music Program 🎧 Audio Program 📼 Videocassette ➴ Internet Resources		
	OBJECTIVES **1.** Describe the factors that contributed to the growth of American imperialism. **2.** Discuss how the United States expanded its economic and political influence in the late 1800s.		
	FOCUS MENU	**SUGGESTED TIME RANGES**	**SUGGESTED LEVELS**
	—— Daily Focus Skills Transparency 22–1, TCR 🖋 📁	5–10 minutes	L1
	—— Preteaching Vocabulary, TWE, p. 638	5–10 minutes	All levels
	—— History Online Chapter 22 Overview ➴	15–20 minutes	All levels
	—— Audio Program Chapter 22 🎧	20–25 minutes	All levels
	TEACH MENU **Guided Practice**		
	—— Time Line Activity, TWE, p. 637	5–10 minutes	All levels
	—— Activity, TWE, p. 639	5–10 minutes	L1
	—— Cooperative Learning Activity, TWE, p. 639	40–60 minutes	ELL, L1
	—— Meeting Special Needs, TWE, p. 640	25–35 minutes	L1
	—— Graphic Organizer Transparency Strategy and Activity 22, TCR 🖋 📁	15–20 minutes	L2
	—— Why It Matters Chapter Transparency Strategy and Activity 22, TCR 🖋 📁	25–30 minutes	All levels
	Independent Practice		
	—— Guided Reading Activity 22–1, TCR 📁	15–20 minutes	ELL, L1
	—— Reading and Study Skills Foldable, p. 637	10–15 minutes	All levels
	ASSESS MENU **Evaluate**		
	—— Section Quiz 22–1, TCR 📁	10–15 minutes	All levels
	—— Interactive Tutor Self-Assessment CD-ROM 💿	20–30 minutes	All levels
	—— ExamView® Pro Testmaker CD-ROM 💿	15–20 minutes	All levels
	Reteach		
	—— Reteaching Activity 22–1, TCR 📁	15–20 minutes	ELL, L1
	—— Reading Essentials and Study Guide 22–1, TCR 📁	25–35 minutes	ELL, L1
	Enrich		
	—— Enrichment Activity 22–1, TCR 📁	10–15 minutes	L2, L3
	—— Linking Past and Present Activity 22, TCR 📁	15–20 minutes	All levels
	CLOSE MENU		
	—— Close, TWE, p. 641	10–15 minutes	All levels

See Optional Resources menu on page viii.

REPRODUCIBLE LESSON PLAN **22–2**

Imperialism in the Pacific   Section 2 *(pp. 644–648)*

LOCAL OBJECTIVES	TWE—Teacher Wraparound Edition TCR—Teacher Classroom Resources
	📁 Blackline Master ✍ Transparency 💿 CD-ROM ◉ DVD 📙 Poster
	🎵 Music Program 🎧 Audio Program 📼 Videocassette ➤ Internet Resources

	OBJECTIVES		
	1. Summarize how the United States gained control of Hawaii and Samoa.		
	2. Explain how competition for influence in China and the Pacific region led to new foreign policies.		

	FOCUS MENU	**SUGGESTED TIME RANGES**	**SUGGESTED LEVELS**
	____ Daily Focus Skills Transparency 22–2, TCR ✍ 📁	5–10 minutes	L1
	____ Preteaching Vocabulary, TWE, p. 644	5–10 minutes	All levels
	____ Audio Program Chapter 22 🎧	20–25 minutes	All levels

	TEACH MENU		
	Guided Practice		
	____ Activity, TWE, p. 645	5–10 minutes	ELL, L1
	____ Cooperative Learning Activity, TWE, p. 645	40–60 minutes	L2
	____ Meeting Special Needs, TWE, p. 646	25–35 minutes	L1
	____ Interdisciplinary Connections Activity, TWE, p. 647	20–30 minutes	L2
	____ Graphic Organizer Transparencies Strategies and Activities, TCR ✍ 📁	20–25 minutes	All levels
	Independent Practice		
	____ Guided Reading Activity 22–2, TCR 📁	15–20 minutes	ELL, L1

	ASSESS MENU		
	Evaluate		
	____ Section Quiz 22–2, TCR 📁	10–15 minutes	All levels
	____ Interactive Tutor Self-Assessment CD-ROM 💿	20–30 minutes	All levels
	____ ExamView® Pro Testmaker CD-ROM 💿	15–20 minutes	All levels
	Reteach		
	____ Reteaching Activity 22–2, TCR 📁	15–20 minutes	ELL, L1
	____ Reading Essentials and Study Guide 22–2, TCR 📁	25–35 minutes	ELL, L1
	Enrich		
	____ Enrichment Activity 22–2, TCR 📁	10–15 minutes	L2, L3

	CLOSE MENU		
	____ Close, TWE, p. 648	10–15 minutes	All levels

See Optional Resources menu on page viii.

Spanish-American War

Section 3 (pp. 649–654)

LOCAL OBJECTIVES	TWE—Teacher Wraparound Edition TCR—Teacher Classroom Resources
	📁 Blackline Master 🖌 Transparency 💿 CD-ROM ⊙ DVD 📄 Poster
	🚩 Music Program 🔊 Audio Program 📼 Videocassette ●⌐ Internet Resources

OBJECTIVES

1. Explain why the Spanish-American War began.

2. Discuss how the United States's role in global affairs grew after the war.

FOCUS MENU	SUGGESTED TIME RANGES	SUGGESTED LEVELS
—— Daily Focus Skills Transparency 22–3, TCR 🖌 📁	5–10 minutes	L1
—— Preteaching Vocabulary, TWE, p. 649	5–10 minutes	All levels
—— Audio Program Chapter 22 🔊	20–25 minutes	All levels

TEACH MENU

Guided Practice

—— Activity, TWE, p. 650	5–10 minutes	L1
—— Cooperative Learning Activity, TWE, p. 650	40–60 minutes	L2
—— Meeting Special Needs, TWE, p. 651	25–35 minutes	L1
—— Interdisciplinary Connections Activity, TWE, p. 652	20–30 minutes	L2
—— Critical Thinking Activity, TWE, p. 653	20–25 minutes	L3
—— Graphic Organizer Transparencies Strategies and Activities, TCR 🖌 📁	20–25 minutes	All levels

Independent Practice

—— Guided Reading Activity 22–3, TCR 📁	15–20 minutes	ELL, L1

ASSESS MENU

Evaluate

—— Section Quiz 22–3, TCR 📁	10–15 minutes	All levels
—— Interactive Tutor Self-Assessment CD-ROM 💿	20–30 minutes	All levels
—— ExamView® Pro Testmaker CD-ROM 💿	15–20 minutes	All levels

Reteach

—— Reteaching Activity 22–3, TCR 📁	15–20 minutes	ELL, L1
—— Reading Essentials and Study Guide 22–3, TCR 📁	25–35 minutes	ELL, L1

Enrich

—— Enrichment Activity 22–3, TCR 📁	10–15 minutes	L2, L3
—— Primary Source Reading 22, TCR 📁	20–30 minutes	All levels

CLOSE MENU

—— Close, TWE, p. 654	10–15 minutes	All levels

See Optional Resources menu on page viii.

Grade ____________ Class(es) ____________ Date ____________ M Tu W Th F

Teacher's Name ______________________________ Date ____________

REPRODUCIBLE LESSON PLAN 22–4

Latin American Policies

Section 4 *(pp. 656–661)*

LOCAL OBJECTIVES	TWE—Teacher Wraparound Edition; TCR—Teacher Classroom Resources; Blackline Master; Transparency; CD-ROM; DVD; Poster; Music Program; Audio Program; Videocassette; Internet Resources		
	OBJECTIVES **1.** Explain what shaped the policies that the United States followed in Latin America. **2.** Describe where and how the United States intervened in Latin America.		
	FOCUS MENU	**SUGGESTED TIME RANGES**	**SUGGESTED LEVELS**
	___ Daily Focus Skills Transparency 22–4, TCR	5–10 minutes	L1
	___ Vocabulary PuzzleMaker CD-ROM	5–10 minutes	All levels
	___ Audio Program Chapter 22	20–25 minutes	All levels
	TEACH MENU		
	Guided Practice		
	___ Activity, TWE, p. 657	5–10 minutes	L1
	___ Cooperative Learning Activity, TWE, p. 657	40–60 minutes	L2
	___ Meeting Special Needs, TWE, p. 658	25–35 minutes	L1
	___ Interdisciplinary Connections Activity, TWE, p. 659	20–30 minutes	L2
	___ Critical Thinking Activity, TWE, p. 660	20–25 minutes	L2
	___ Graphic Organizer Transparencies Strategies and Activities, TCR	20–25 minutes	All levels
	Independent Practice		
	___ Guided Reading Activity 22–4 TCR	15–20 minutes	ELL, L1
	___ Vocabulary Activity 22, TCR	20–30 minutes	All levels
	___ Chapter Skills Activity 22, TCR	40–60 minutes	All levels
	___ Critical Thinking Activity 22, TCR	15–20 minutes	L2, L3
	___ Geography and History Activity 22, TCR	20–30 minutes	L1
	___ Time Line Activity 22, TCR	15–20 minutes	All levels
	ASSESS MENU		
	Evaluate		
	___ Section Quiz 22–4, TCR	10–15 minutes	All levels
	___ Performance Assessment Activity 22, TCR	25–30 minutes	All levels
	___ Interactive Tutor Self-Assessment CD-ROM	20–30 minutes	All levels
	___ ExamView® Pro Testmaker CD-ROM	15–20 minutes	All levels
	___ History Online Activity	15–20 minutes	All levels
	Reteach		
	___ Reteaching Activity 22–4, TCR	15–20 minutes	ELL, L1
	___ Reading Essentials and Study Guide 22–4, TCR	25–35 minutes	ELL, L1
	___ Take-Home Review Activity 22, TCR	10–15 minutes	All levels
	___ MindJogger Videoquiz, Chapter 22	20–25 minutes	All levels
	Enrich		
	___ Enrichment Activity 22–4, TCR	10–15 minutes	L2, L3
	CLOSE MENU		
	___ Close, TWE, p. 661	10–15 minutes	All levels

See Optional Resources menu on page viii.

War in Europe

Section 1 (pp. 666–670)

LOCAL OBJECTIVES	TWE—Teacher Wraparound Edition 📁 Blackline Master 🖫 Transparency 📻 Music Program 🔊 Audio Program	TCR—Teacher Classroom Resources 💿 CD-ROM 📀 DVD 📖 Poster 📼 Videocassette 🖇 Internet Resources

OBJECTIVES

1. Understand the factors that led to World War I.
2. Describe how the early fighting progressed in Europe.

FOCUS MENU	**SUGGESTED TIME RANGES**	**SUGGESTED LEVELS**
____ Daily Focus Skills Transparency 23–1, TCR 🖫 📁	5–10 minutes	L1
____ Preteaching Vocabulary, TWE, p. 666	5–10 minutes	All levels
____ History Online Chapter 23 Overview 🖇	15–20 minutes	All levels
____ Audio Program Chapter 23 🔊	20–25 minutes	All levels

TEACH MENU
Guided Practice

____ Time Line Activity, TWE, p. 665	10–15 minutes	All levels
____ Activity, TWE, p. 667	5–10 minutes	L1
____ Cooperative Learning Activity, TWE, p. 667	40–60 minutes	L2
____ Meeting Special Needs, TWE, p. 668	25–35 minutes	L1
____ Interdisciplinary Connections Activity, TWE, p. 669	20–30 minutes	L1
____ Graphic Organizer Transparencies Strategies and Activities, TCR 🖫 📁	20–25 minutes	All levels

Independent Practice

____ Guided Reading Activity 23–1, TCR 📁	15–20 minutes	ELL, L1
____ Reading and Study Skills Foldable, p. 665	10–15 minutes	All levels

ASSESS MENU
Evaluate

____ Section Quiz 23–1, TCR 📁	10–15 minutes	All levels
____ Interactive Tutor Self-Assessment CD-ROM 💿	20–30 minutes	All levels
____ ExamView® Pro Testmaker CD-ROM 💿	15–20 minutes	All levels

Reteach

____ Reteaching Activity 23–1, TCR 📁	15–20 minutes	ELL, L1
____ Reading Essentials and Study Guide 23–1, TCR 📁	25–35 minutes	ELL, L1

Enrich

____ Enrichment Activity 23–1, TCR 📁	10–15 minutes	L2, L3

CLOSE MENU

____ Close, TWE, p. 670	10–15 minutes	All levels

See Optional Resources menu on page viii.

America's Road to War

Section 2 *(pp. 671–676)*

LOCAL OBJECTIVES	TWE—Teacher Wraparound Edition TCR—Teacher Classroom Resources 📁 Blackline Master ⬚ Transparency 🔘 CD-ROM 🔘 DVD 📙 Poster 🎵 Music Program 🔊 Audio Program 📼 Videocassette 🔗 Internet Resources

	OBJECTIVES		
	1. Describe how Americans responded to the war in Europe.		
	2. Explain what led to American involvement in the war.		

	FOCUS MENU	**SUGGESTED TIME RANGES**	**SUGGESTED LEVELS**
	____ Daily Focus Skills Transparency 23–2, TCR ⬚ 📁	5–10 minutes	L1
	____ Preteaching Vocabulary, TWE, p. 671	5–10 minutes	All levels
	____ Audio Program Chapter 23 🔊	20–25 minutes	All levels

	TEACH MENU		
	Guided Practice		
	____ Activity, TWE, p. 672	5–10 minutes	L1
	____ Cooperative Learning Activity, TWE, p. 672	40–60 minutes	L2
	____ Meeting Special Needs, TWE, p. 673	25–35 minutes	L1
	____ Interdisciplinary Connections Activity, TWE, p. 674	20–30 minutes	L1
	____ Critical Thinking Activity, TWE, p. 675	20–25 minutes	L2
	____ Graphic Organizer Transparency Strategy and Activity 23, TCR ⬚ 📁	15–20 minutes	L2
	Independent Practice		
	____ Guided Reading Activity 23–2, TCR 📁	15–20 minutes	ELL, L1

	ASSESS MENU		
	Evaluate		
	____ Section Quiz 23–2, TCR 📁	10–15 minutes	All levels
	____ Interactive Tutor Self-Assessment CD-ROM 🔘	20–30 minutes	All levels
	____ ExamView® Pro Testmaker CD-ROM 🔘	15–20 minutes	All levels
	____ History Online Activity 🔗	15–20 minutes	All levels
	Reteach		
	____ Reteaching Activity 23–2, TCR 📁	15–20 minutes	ELL, L1
	____ Reading Essentials and Study Guide 23–2, TCR 📁	25–35 minutes	ELL, L1
	Enrich		
	____ Enrichment Activity 23–2, TCR 📁	10–15 minutes	L2, L3

	CLOSE MENU		
	____ Close, TWE, p. 676	10–15 minutes	All levels

See Optional Resources menu on page viii.

Americans Join the Allies   Section 3 *(pp. 677–681)*

LOCAL OBJECTIVES	TWE—Teacher Wraparound Edition TCR—Teacher Classroom Resources 📁 Blackline Master 🖌 Transparency 💿 CD-ROM 💿 DVD 📕 Poster 🎵 Music Program 🔊 Audio Program 📼 Videocassette 🔗 Internet Resources

OBJECTIVES

1. Describe what was happening in Europe when the United States entered the war.

2. Understand the role American troops played in the fighting.

FOCUS MENU	SUGGESTED TIME RANGES	SUGGESTED LEVELS
—— Daily Focus Skills Transparency 23, TCR 🖌 📁	5–10 minutes	L1
—— Preteaching Vocabulary, TWE, p. 677	5–10 minutes	All levels
—— Audio Program Chapter 23 🔊	20–25 minutes	All levels

TEACH MENU		
Guided Practice		
—— Activity, TWE, p. 678	5–10 minutes	L1
—— Cooperative Learning Activity, TWE, p. 678	40–60 minutes	L2
—— Meeting Special Needs, TWE, p. 679	25–35 minutes	L1
—— Interdisciplinary Connections Activity, TWE, p. 680	20–30 minutes	L2
—— Graphic Organizer Transparencies Strategies and Activities, TCR 🖌 📁	20–25 minutes	All levels
—— Why It Matters Chapter Transparency Strategy and Activity 23, TCR 🖌 📁	25–30 minutes	All levels
Independent Practice		
—— Guided Reading Activity 23–3, TCR 📁	15–20 minutes	ELL, L1

ASSESS MENU		
Evaluate		
—— Section Quiz 23–3, TCR 📁	10–15 minutes	All levels
—— Interactive Tutor Self-Assessment CD-ROM 💿	20–30 minutes	All levels
—— ExamView® Pro Testmaker CD-ROM 💿	15–20 minutes	All levels
Reteach		
—— Reteaching Activity 23–3, TCR 📁	15–20 minutes	ELL, L1
—— Reading Essentials and Study Guide 23–3, TCR 📁	25–35 minutes	ELL, L1
Enrich		
—— Enrichment Activity 23–3, TCR 📁	10–15 minutes	L2, L3
—— Linking Past and Present Activity 23, TCR 📁	20–30 minutes	All levels

CLOSE MENU		
—— Close, TWE, p. 681	10–15 minutes	All levels

See Optional Resources menu on page viii.

The War at Home

Section 4 (pp. 683–686)

LOCAL OBJECTIVES	TWE—Teacher Wraparound Edition TCR—Teacher Classroom Resources
	📁 Blackline Master 🎚 Transparency ⊙ CD-ROM ⊙ DVD 📕 Poster
	🎵 Music Program 🔊 Audio Program 📼 Videocassette ⟿ Internet Resources

	OBJECTIVES		
	1. Describe the steps the United States took to organize and prepare for World War I.		
	2. Explain how the war affected Americans.		

	FOCUS MENU	**SUGGESTED TIME RANGES**	**SUGGESTED LEVELS**
	—— Daily Focus Skills Transparency 23–4, TCR 🎚 📁	5–10 minutes	L1
	—— Preteaching Vocabulary, TWE, p. 683	5–10 minutes	All levels
	—— Audio Program Chapter 23 🔊	20–25 minutes	All levels

	TEACH MENU		
	Guided Practice		
	—— Activity, TWE, p. 684	5–10 minutes	L1
	—— Cooperative Learning Activity, TWE, p. 684	40–60 minutes	L2
	—— Meeting Special Needs, TWE, p. 685	25–35 minutes	L1
	—— Graphic Organizer Transparencies Strategies and Activities, TCR 🎚 📁	20–25 minutes	All levels
	Independent Practice		
	—— Guided Reading Activity 23–4, TCR 📁	15–20 minutes	ELL, L1

	ASSESS MENU		
	Evaluate		
	—— Section Quiz 23–4, TCR 📁	10–15 minutes	All levels
	—— Interactive Tutor Self-Assessment CD-ROM ⊙	20–30 minutes	All levels
	—— ExamView® Pro Testmaker CD-ROM ⊙	15–20 minutes	All levels
	Reteach		
	—— Reteaching Activity 23–4, TCR 📁	15–20 minutes	ELL, L1
	—— Reading Essentials and Study Guide 23–4, TCR 📁	25–35 minutes	ELL, L1
	Enrich		
	—— Enrichment Activity 23–4, TCR 📁	10–15 minutes	L2, L3

	CLOSE MENU		
	—— Close, TWE, p. 686	10–15 minutes	All levels

See Optional Resources menu on page viii.

Grade ＿＿＿＿＿＿ Class(es) ＿＿＿＿＿＿ Date ＿＿＿＿＿＿ M Tu W Th F

Teacher's Name ＿＿＿＿＿＿＿＿＿＿＿＿＿＿＿＿＿＿ Date ＿＿＿＿＿

Searching for Peace

Section 5 *(pp. 688–691)*

LOCAL OBJECTIVES	TWE—Teacher Wraparound Edition TCR—Teacher Classroom Resources
	📁 Blackline Master 🖋 Transparency 💿 CD-ROM 💿 DVD 📕 Poster
	🎵 Music Program 🔊 Audio Program 📼 Videocassette 🔗 Internet Resources

	OBJECTIVES **1.** Examine the principles Woodrow Wilson proposed as the basis for world peace. **2.** Explain why many Americans opposed the Treaty of Versailles.		
	FOCUS MENU	**SUGGESTED TIME RANGES**	**SUGGESTED LEVELS**
	—— Daily Focus Skills Transparency 23–5, TCR 🖋 📁	5–10 minutes	L1
	—— Vocabulary PuzzleMaker CD-ROM 💿	5–10 minutes	All levels
	—— Audio Program Chapter 23 🔊	20–25 minutes	All levels
	TEACH MENU **Guided Practice**		
	—— Activity, TWE, p. 689	5–10 minutes	L1
	—— Cooperative Learning Activity, TWE, p. 689	40–60 minutes	L2
	—— Meeting Special Needs, TWE, p. 690	25–35 minutes	L1
	—— Graphic Organizer Transparencies Strategies and Activities, TCR 🖋 📁	20–25 minutes	All levels
	Independent Practice		
	—— Guided Reading Activity 23–5 TCR 📁	15–20 minutes	ELL, L1
	—— Vocabulary Activity 23, TCR 📁	20–30 minutes	All levels
	—— Chapter Skills Activity 23, TCR 📁	40–60 minutes	L2
	—— Critical Thinking Activity 23, TCR 📁	15–20 minutes	L2
	—— Geography and History Activity 23, TCR 📁	15–20 minutes	All levels
	—— Time Line Activity 23, TCR 📁	15–20 minutes	All levels
	ASSESS MENU **Evaluate**		
	—— Section Quiz 23–5, TCR 📁	10–15 minutes	All levels
	—— Performance Assessment Activity 23, TCR 📁	25–30 minutes	All levels
	—— Interactive Tutor Self-Assessment CD-ROM 💿	20–30 minutes	All levels
	—— ExamView® Pro Testmaker CD-ROM 💿	15–20 minutes	All levels
	Reteach		
	—— Reteaching Activity 23–5, TCR 📁	15–20 minutes	ELL, L1
	—— Reading Essentials and Study Guide 23–5, TCR 📁	25–35 minutes	ELL, L1
	—— Take-Home Review Activity 23, TCR 📁	10–15 minutes	All levels
	—— MindJogger Videoquiz, Chapter 23 💿 📼	20–25 minutes	All levels
	Enrich		
	—— Enrichment Activity 23–5, TCR 📁	10–15 minutes	L2, L3
	—— Primary Source Reading 23, TCR 📁	15–20 minutes	All levels
	CLOSE MENU		
	—— Close, TWE, p. 691	10–15 minutes	All levels

See Optional Resources menu on page viii.

Time of Turmoil

Section 1 *(pp. 700–703)*

LOCAL OBJECTIVES	TWE—Teacher Wraparound Edition TCR—Teacher Classroom Resources 🗀 Blackline Master ⚒ Transparency 💿 CD-ROM ⊙ DVD 🖵 Poster 🏁 Music Program 🔊 Audio Program 📼 Videocassette ➴ Internet Resources

OBJECTIVES

1. Identify the factors that contributed to prejudice toward foreigners.

2. Understand how the labor and racial unrest of the 1920s affected the nation.

FOCUS MENU	**SUGGESTED TIME RANGES**	**SUGGESTED LEVELS**
___ Daily Focus Skills Transparency 24–1, TCR ⚒ 🗀	5–10 minutes	L1
___ Preteaching Vocabulary, TWE, p. 700	5–10 minutes	All levels
___ History Online Chapter 24 Overview ➴	15–20 minutes	All levels
___ Audio Program Chapter 24 🔊	20–25 minutes	All levels

TEACH MENU

Guided Practice

___ Time Line Activity, TWE, p. 699	15–20 minutes	L1
___ Activity, TWE, p. 701	5–10 minutes	L1
___ Cooperative Learning Activity, TWE, p. 701	40–60 minutes	L2
___ Meeting Special Needs, TWE, p. 702	25–35 minutes	L1
___ Graphic Organizer Transparencies Strategies and Activities, TCR ⚒ 🗀	20–25 minutes	All levels

Independent Practice

___ Guided Reading Activity 24–1, TCR 🗀	15–20 minutes	ELL, L1
___ Reading and Study Skills Foldable, p. 699	10–15 minutes	All levels

ASSESS MENU

Evaluate

___ Section Quiz 24–1, TCR 🗀	10–15 minutes	All levels
___ Interactive Tutor Self-Assessment CD-ROM 💿	20–30 minutes	All levels
___ ExamView® Pro Testmaker CD-ROM 💿	15–20 minutes	All levels

Reteach

___ Reteaching Activity 24–1, TCR 🗀	15–20 minutes	ELL, L1
___ Reading Essentials and Study Guide 24–1, TCR 🗀	25–35 minutes	ELL, L1

Enrich

___ Enrichment Activity 24–1, TCR 🗀	10–15 minutes	L2, L3
___ Primary Source Reading 24, TCR 🗀	20–30 minutes	All levels

CLOSE MENU

___ Close, TWE, p. 703	10–15 minutes	All levels

See Optional Resources menu on page viii.

Desire for Normalcy

Section 2 *(pp. 704–707)*

LOCAL OBJECTIVES	TWE—Teacher Wraparound Edition TCR—Teacher Classroom Resources 📁 Blackline Master 🖌 Transparency 🔘 CD-ROM 🔘 DVD 📖 Poster 🎵 Music Program 🔊 Audio Program 📼 Videocassette 🔗 Internet Resources		
	OBJECTIVES **1.** Analyze the problems that faced the Harding presidency. **2.** Compare and contrast the policies Presidents Harding and Coolidge followed in business and foreign affairs.		
	FOCUS MENU	**SUGGESTED TIME RANGES**	**SUGGESTED LEVELS**
	—— Daily Focus Skills Transparency 24–2, TCR 🖌 📁	5–10 minutes	L1
	—— Preteaching Vocabulary, TWE, p. 704	5–10 minutes	All levels
	—— Audio Program Chapter 24 🔊	20–25 minutes	All levels
	TEACH MENU **Guided Practice**		
	—— Activity, TWE, p. 705	5–10 minutes	L2
	—— Cooperative Learning Activity, TWE, p. 705	40–60 minutes	L2
	—— Meeting Special Needs, TWE, p. 706	25–35 minutes	L1
	—— Graphic Organizer Transparency Strategy and Activity 24, TCR 🖌 📁	15–20 minutes	L2
	Independent Practice		
	—— Guided Reading Activity 24–2, TCR 📁	15–20 minutes	ELL, L1
	ASSESS MENU **Evaluate**		
	—— Section Quiz 24–2, TCR 📁	10–15 minutes	All levels
	—— Interactive Tutor Self-Assessment CD-ROM 🔘	20–30 minutes	All levels
	—— ExamView® Pro Testmaker CD-ROM 🔘	15–20 minutes	All levels
	Reteach		
	—— Reteaching Activity 24–2, TCR 📁	15–20 minutes	ELL, L1
	—— Reading Essentials and Study Guide 24–2, TCR 📁	25–35 minutes	ELL, L1
	Enrich		
	—— Enrichment Activity 24–2, TCR 📁	10–15 minutes	L2, L3
	CLOSE MENU		
	—— Close, TWE, p. 707	10–15 minutes	All levels

See Optional Resources menu on page viii.

A Booming Economy

Section 3 *(pp. 709–712)*

LOCAL OBJECTIVES	TWE—Teacher Wraparound Edition TCR—Teacher Classroom Resources
	📁 Blackline Master 🎛 Transparency 💿 CD-ROM 💿 DVD 📙 Poster
	🚩 Music Program 🎧 Audio Program 📼 Videocassette 🖱 Internet Resources

OBJECTIVES

1. Describe how the prosperity of the 1920s affected the nation.

2. Summarize the impact the automobile had on American life.

FOCUS MENU	SUGGESTED TIME RANGES	SUGGESTED LEVELS
—— Daily Focus Skills Transparency 24–3, TCR 🎛 📁	5–10 minutes	L1
—— Preteaching Vocabulary, TWE, p. 709	5–10 minutes	All levels
—— Audio Program Chapter 24 🎧	20–25 minutes	All levels

TEACH MENU		
Guided Practice		
—— Activity, TWE, p. 710	5–10 minutes	L1
—— Cooperative Learning Activity, TWE, p. 710	40–60 minutes	L2
—— Meeting Special Needs, TWE, p. 711	25–35 minutes	L1
—— Graphic Organizer Transparencies		
Strategies and Activities, TCR 🎛 📁	20–25 minutes	All levels
Independent Practice		
—— Guided Reading Activity 24–3, TCR 📁	15–20 minutes	ELL, L1

ASSESS MENU		
Evaluate		
—— Section Quiz 24–3, TCR 📁	10–15 minutes	All levels
—— Interactive Tutor Self-Assessment CD-ROM 💿	20–30 minutes	All levels
—— ExamView® Pro Testmaker CD-ROM 💿	15–20 minutes	All levels
—— History Online Activity 🖱	15–20 minutes	All levels
Reteach		
—— Reteaching Activity 24–3, TCR 📁	15–20 minutes	ELL, L1
—— Reading Essentials and Study Guide 24–3, TCR 📁	25–35 minutes	ELL, L1
Enrich		
—— Enrichment Activity 24–3, TCR 📁	10–15 minutes	L2, L3

CLOSE MENU		
—— Close, TWE, p. 712	10–15 minutes	All levels

See Optional Resources menu on page viii.

Grade _____ Class(es) _____ Date _____ M Tu W Th F

Teacher's Name _____ Date _____

The Roaring Twenties   Section 4 *(pp. 713–719)*

LOCAL OBJECTIVES	TWE—Teacher Wraparound Edition TCR—Teacher Classroom Resources Blackline Master Transparency CD-ROM DVD Poster Music Program Audio Program Videocassette Internet Resources		
	OBJECTIVES **1.** Explore how lifestyles in America changed in the 1920s. **2.** Explain the cultural clashes that occurred in the United States in the 1920s.		
	FOCUS MENU	**SUGGESTED TIME RANGES**	**SUGGESTED LEVELS**
	—— Daily Focus Skills Transparency 24–4, TCR	5–10 minutes	L1
	—— Vocabulary PuzzleMaker CD-ROM	5–10 minutes	All levels
	—— Audio Program Chapter 24	20–25 minutes	All levels
	TEACH MENU **Guided Practice**		
	—— Activity, TWE, p. 714	5–10 minutes	L1
	—— Cooperative Learning Activity, TWE, p. 714	40–60 minutes	L2
	—— Meeting Special Needs, TWE, p. 715	25–35 minutes	L1
	—— Interdisciplinary Connections Activity, TWE, p. 716	20–30 minutes	L2
	—— Critical Thinking Activity, TWE, p. 717	20–25 minutes	L3
	—— Extending the Content, TWE, p. 718	5–10 minutes	L3
	—— Graphic Organizer Transparencies Strategies and Activities, TCR	20–25 minutes	All levels
	—— Why It Matters Chapter Transparency Strategy and Activity 24, TCR	25–30 minutes	All levels
	Independent Practice		
	—— Guided Reading Activity 24–4 TCR	15–20 minutes	ELL, L1
	—— Vocabulary Activity 24, TCR	20–30 minutes	All levels
	—— Chapter Skills Activity 24, TCR	40–60 minutes	L2
	—— Critical Thinking Activity 24, TCR	20–30 minutes	L1
	—— Geography and History Activity 24, TCR	15–20 minutes	All levels
	—— Time Line Activity 24, TCR	15–20 minutes	L1
	ASSESS MENU **Evaluate**		
	—— Section Quiz 24–4, TCR	10–15 minutes	All levels
	—— Performance Assessment Activity 24, TCR	25–30 minutes	All levels
	—— Interactive Tutor Self-Assessment CD-ROM	20–30 minutes	All levels
	—— ExamView® Pro Testmaker CD-ROM	15–20 minutes	All levels
	Reteach		
	—— Reteaching Activity 24–4, TCR	15–20 minutes	ELL, L1
	—— Reading Essentials and Study Guide 24–4, TCR	25–35 minutes	ELL, L1
	—— Take-Home Review Activity 24, TCR	10–15 minutes	All levels
	—— MindJogger Videoquiz, Chapter 24	20–25 minutes	All levels
	Enrich		
	—— Enrichment Activity 24–4, TCR	10–15 minutes	L2, L3
	—— Linking Past and Present Activity 24, TCR	15–20 minutes	All levels
	CLOSE MENU		
	—— Close, TWE, p. 719	10–15 minutes	All levels

See Optional Resources menu on page viii.

The American Journey

The Great Depression

Section 1 *(pp. 724–728)*

LOCAL OBJECTIVES	TWE—Teacher Wraparound Edition 　　　 TCR—Teacher Classroom Resources
	📁 Blackline Master 　🖐 Transparency 　🔘 CD-ROM 　◉ DVD 　📕 Poster
	🎵 Music Program 　🔊 Audio Program 　📼 Videocassette 　�'⁵ Internet Resources

OBJECTIVES

1. Examine the causes behind the stock market crash.
2. Explain how the Great Depression plunged many Americans into poverty.
3. Describe how Hoover reacted to the Great Depression.

		SUGGESTED TIME RANGES	SUGGESTED LEVELS
	FOCUS MENU		
	—— Daily Focus Skills Transparency 25–1, TCR 🖐 📁	5–10 minutes	L1
	—— Preteaching Vocabulary, TWE, p. 724	5–10 minutes	All levels
	—— History Online Chapter 25 Overview ➝⁵	15–20 minutes	All levels
	—— Audio Program Chapter 25 🔊	20–25 minutes	All levels
	TEACH MENU		
	Guided Practice		
	—— Time Line Activity, TWE, p. 723	10–15 minutes	All levels
	—— Activity, TWE, p. 725	5–10 minutes	L1
	—— Cooperative Learning Activity, TWE, p. 725	40–60 minutes	L1
	—— Meeting Special Needs, TWE, p. 726	25–35 minutes	L1
	—— Interdisciplinary Connections Activity, TWE, p. 727	20–30 minutes	L2
	—— Graphic Organizer Transparencies Strategies and Activities, TCR 🖐 📁	20–25 minutes	All levels
	—— Why It Matters Chapter Transparency Strategy and Activity 25, TCR 🖐 📁	25–30 minutes	All levels
	Independent Practice		
	—— Guided Reading Activity 25–1, TCR 📁	15–20 minutes	ELL, L1
	—— Reading and Study Skills Foldable, p. 723	10–15 minutes	All levels
	ASSESS MENU		
	Evaluate		
	—— Section Quiz 25–1, TCR 📁	10–15 minutes	All levels
	—— Interactive Tutor Self-Assessment CD-ROM 🔘	20–30 minutes	All levels
	—— ExamView® Pro Testmaker CD-ROM 🔘	15–20 minutes	All levels
	Reteach		
	—— Reteaching Activity 25–1, TCR 📁	15–20 minutes	ELL, L1
	—— Reading Essentials and Study Guide 25–1, TCR 📁	25–35 minutes	ELL, L1
	Enrich		
	—— Enrichment Activity 25–1, TCR 📁	10–15 minutes	L2, L3
	CLOSE MENU		
	—— Close, TWE, p. 728	10–15 minutes	All levels

See Optional Resources menu on page viii.

Roosevelt's New Deal

Section 2 (pp. 729–734)

LOCAL OBJECTIVES	TWE—Teacher Wraparound Edition TCR—Teacher Classroom Resources 📁 Blackline Master 🖌 Transparency 💿 CD-ROM 📀 DVD 📕 Poster 🎵 Music Program 🎧 Audio Program 📼 Videocassette 🌐 Internet Resources		
	OBJECTIVES **1.** Identify how Roosevelt tried to restore the confidence of the American people. **2.** Explore the programs that were created in Roosevelt's first 100 days as president.		
	FOCUS MENU	**SUGGESTED TIME RANGES**	**SUGGESTED LEVELS**
	—— Daily Focus Skills Transparency 25–2, TCR 🖌 📁	5–10 minutes	L1
	—— Preteaching Vocabulary, TWE, p. 729	5–10 minutes	All levels
	—— Audio Program Chapter 25 🎧	20–25 minutes	All levels
	TEACH MENU **Guided Practice**		
	—— Activity, TWE, p. 730	5–10 minutes	ELL, L1
	—— Cooperative Learning Activity, TWE, p. 730	40–60 minutes	L2
	—— Meeting Special Needs, TWE, p. 731	25–35 minutes	L1
	—— Interdisciplinary Connections Activity, TWE, p. 732	20–30 minutes	L2
	—— Critical Thinking Activity, TWE, p. 733	20–25 minutes	L3
	—— Graphic Organizer Transparency Strategy and Activity 25, TCR 🖌 📁	15–20 minutes	L2
	—— Why It Matters Chapter Transparency Strategy and Activity 25, TCR 🖌 📁	25–30 minutes	All levels
	Independent Practice		
	—— Guided Reading Activity 25–2, TCR 📁	15–20 minutes	ELL, L1
	ASSESS MENU **Evaluate**		
	—— Section Quiz 25–2, TCR 📁	10–15 minutes	All levels
	—— Interactive Tutor Self-Assessment CD-ROM 💿	20–30 minutes	All levels
	—— ExamView® Pro Testmaker CD-ROM 💿	15–20 minutes	All levels
	Reteach		
	—— Reteaching Activity 25–2, TCR 📁	15–20 minutes	ELL, L1
	—— Reading Essentials and Study Guide 25–2, TCR 📁	25–35 minutes	ELL, L1
	Enrich		
	—— Enrichment Activity 25–2, TCR 📁	10–15 minutes	L2, L3
	—— Linking Past and Present Activity 25, TCR 📁	15–20 minutes	All levels
	CLOSE MENU		
	—— Close, TWE, p. 734	10–15 minutes	All levels

See Optional Resources menu on page viii.

Grade _____ Class(es) _____ Date _____ M Tu W Th F

Teacher's Name _____ Date _____

REPRODUCIBLE LESSON PLAN 25–3

Life During the Depression

Section 3 *(pp. 735–739)*

LOCAL OBJECTIVES	TWE—Teacher Wraparound Edition　　TCR—Teacher Classroom Resources 📁 Blackline Master　🎛 Transparency　💿 CD-ROM　🔘 DVD　📕 Poster 🎵 Music Program　🔊 Audio Program　📼 Videocassette　🔗 Internet Resources		
	OBJECTIVES **1.** Explain how the Depression affected minority groups. **2.** Identify what radical political movements gained influence.		
	FOCUS MENU	**SUGGESTED TIME RANGES**	**SUGGESTED LEVELS**
	____ Daily Focus Skills Transparency 25–3, TCR 🎛 📁	5–10 minutes	L1
	____ Preteaching Vocabulary, TWE, p. 735	5–10 minutes	All levels
	____ Audio Program Chapter 25 🔊	20–25 minutes	All levels
	TEACH MENU **Guided Practice**		
	____ Activity, TWE, p. 736	5–10 minutes	L1
	____ Cooperative Learning Activity, TWE, p. 736	40–60 minutes	L2
	____ Meeting Special Needs, TWE, p. 737	25–35 minutes	L1
	____ Interdisciplinary Connections Activity, TWE, p. 738	20–30 minutes	L2
	____ Graphic Organizer Transparencies Strategies and Activities, TCR 🎛 📁	20–25 minutes	All levels
	____ American Art and Architecture 🎛 📁	25–30 minutes	All levels
	Independent Practice		
	____ Guided Reading Activity 25–3, TCR 📁	15–20 minutes	ELL, L1
	ASSESS MENU **Evaluate**		
	____ Section Quiz 25–3, TCR 📁	10–15 minutes	All levels
	____ Interactive Tutor Self-Assessment CD-ROM 💿	20–30 minutes	All levels
	____ ExamView® Pro Testmaker CD-ROM 💿	15–20 minutes	All levels
	Reteach		
	____ Reteaching Activity 25–3, TCR 📁	15–20 minutes	ELL, L1
	____ Reading Essentials and Study Guide 25–3, TCR 📁	25–35 minutes	ELL, L1
	Enrich		
	____ Enrichment Activity 25–3, TCR 📁	10–15 minutes	L2, L3
	____ Primary Source Reading 25, TCR 📁	20-30 minutes	All levels
	CLOSE MENU		
	____ Close, TWE, p. 739	10–15 minutes	All levels

See Optional Resources menu on page viii.

Copyright © by The McGraw-Hill Companies, Inc.

The American Journey

Effects of the New Deal   Section 4 (pp. 742–746)

LOCAL OBJECTIVES	TWE—Teacher Wraparound Edition TCR—Teacher Classroom Resources 📁 Blackline Master 🔥 Transparency 💿 CD-ROM 💿 DVD 📒 Poster 🎵 Music Program 🔊 Audio Program 📼 Videocassette ⬤ᶴ Internet Resources
	OBJECTIVES **1.** Understand why people criticized Roosevelt and the New Deal. **2.** Examine how the Second New Deal created new economic and social roles for government.

	FOCUS MENU	**SUGGESTED TIME RANGES**	**SUGGESTED LEVELS**
	—— Daily Focus Skills Transparency 25–4, TCR 🔥 📁	5–10 minutes	L1
	—— Vocabulary PuzzleMaker CD-ROM 💿	5–10 minutes	All levels
	—— Audio Program Chapter 25 🔊	20–25 minutes	All levels

	TEACH MENU		
	Guided Practice		
	—— Activity, TWE, p. 743	5–10 minutes	L1
	—— Cooperative Learning Activity, TWE, p. 743	40–60 minutes	L3
	—— Meeting Special Needs, TWE, p. 744	25–35 minutes	L1
	—— Interdisciplinary Connections Activity, TWE, p. 745	20–30 minutes	L2
	—— Graphic Organizer Transparencies Strategies and Activities, TCR 🔥 📁	20–25 minutes	All levels
	Independent Practice		
	—— Guided Reading Activity, 25–4 TCR 📁	15–20 minutes	ELL, L1
	—— Vocabulary Activity 25, TCR 📁	20–30 minutes	All levels
	—— Chapter Skills Activity 25, TCR 📁	40–60 minutes	L2, L3
	—— Critical Thinking Activity 25, TCR 📁	20–30 minutes	L2
	—— Geography and History Activity 25, TCR 📁	15–20 minutes	All levels
	—— Time Line Activity 25, TCR 📁	15–20 minutes	All levels

	ASSESS MENU		
	Evaluate		
	—— Section Quiz 25–4, TCR 📁	10–15 minutes	All levels
	—— Performance Assessment Activity 25, TCR 📁	25–30 minutes	All levels
	—— Interactive Tutor Self-Assessment CD-ROM 💿	20–30 minutes	All levels
	—— ExamView® Pro Testmaker CD-ROM 💿	15–20 minutes	All levels
	—— History Online Activity ⬤ᶴ	15–20 minutes	All levels
	Reteach		
	—— Reteaching Activity 25–4, TCR 📁	15–20 minutes	ELL, L1
	—— Reading Essentials and Study Guide 25–4, TCR 📁	25–35 minutes	ELL, L1
	—— Take-Home Review Activity 25, TCR 📁	10–15 minutes	All levels
	—— MindJogger Videoquiz, Chapter 25 💿 📼	20–25 minutes	All levels
	Enrich		
	—— Enrichment Activity 25–4, TCR 📁	10–15 minutes	L2, L3

	CLOSE MENU		
	—— Close, TWE, p. 746	10–15 minutes	All levels

See Optional Resources menu on page viii.

Road to War

Section 1 *(pp. 752–755)*

LOCAL OBJECTIVES	TWE—Teacher Wraparound Edition TCR—Teacher Classroom Resources 📁 Blackline Master ⚒ Transparency 💿 CD-ROM ⊙ DVD 📕 Poster 🎵 Music Program 🎧 Audio Program 📼 Videocassette 🖥 Internet Resources

	OBJECTIVES **1.** Discuss why dictators came to power around the world. **2.** Describe what actions led to the outbreak of World War II.		

	FOCUS MENU	**SUGGESTED TIME RANGES**	**SUGGESTED LEVELS**
	—— Daily Focus Skills Transparency 26–1, TCR ⚒ 📁	5–10 minutes	L1
	—— Preteaching Vocabulary, TWE, p. 752 ⚒ 📁	5–10 minutes	All levels
	—— History Online Chapter 26 Overview 🖥	15–20 minutes	All levels
	—— Audio Program Chapter 26 🎧	20–25 minutes	All levels

	TEACH MENU **Guided Practice**		
	—— Time Line Activity, TWE, p. 751	5–10 minutes	All levels
	—— Activity, TWE, p. 753	5–10 minutes	L2
	—— Cooperative Learning Activity, TWE, p. 753	40–60 minutes	L1
	—— Meeting Special Needs, TWE, p. 754	25–35 minutes	All levels
	—— Graphic Organizer Transparencies Strategies and Activities, TCR ⚒ 📁	20–25 minutes	Need levels
	Independent Practice		
	—— Guided Reading Activity 26–1, TCR 📁	15–20 minutes	L1
	—— Reading and Study Skills Foldable, p. 751	10–15 minutes	All levels

	ASSESS MENU **Evaluate**		
	—— Section Quiz 26–1, TCR 📁	10–15 minutes	All levels
	—— Interactive Tutor Self-Assessment CD-ROM 💿	20–30 minutes	All levels
	—— ExamView® Pro Testmaker CD-ROM 💿	15–20 minutes	All levels
	Reteach		
	—— Reteaching Activity 26–1, TCR 📁	15–20 minutes	ELL, L1
	—— Reading Essentials and Study Guide 26–1, TCR 📁	25–35 minutes	ELL, L1
	Enrich		
	—— Enrichment Activity 26–1, TCR 📁	10–15 minutes	L2, L3

	CLOSE MENU		
	—— Close, TWE, p. 755	10–15 minutes	All levels

See Optional Resources menu on page viii.

War Begins

Section 2 (pp. 758–763)

LOCAL OBJECTIVES	TWE—Teacher Wraparound Edition TCR—Teacher Classroom Resources 📁 Blackline Master 🔖 Transparency ⊙ CD-ROM ⊙ DVD 📕 Poster 🎵 Music Program 🎧 Audio Program 📼 Videocassette ⟿ Internet Resources		
	OBJECTIVES **1.** Identify which European nations fell to Germany in 1939 and 1940. **2.** Describe how the United States responded to the war in Europe.		
	FOCUS MENU	**SUGGESTED TIME RANGES**	**SUGGESTED LEVELS**
	—— Daily Focus Skills Transparency 26–2, TCR 🔖 📁	5–10 minutes	L1
	—— Preteaching Vocabulary, TWE, p. 758	5–10 minutes	All levels
	—— Audio Program Chapter 26 🎧	20–25 minutes	All levels
	TEACH MENU **Guided Practice**		
	—— Activity, TWE, p. 759	5–10 minutes	L1
	—— Cooperative Learning Activity, TWE, p. 759	40–60 minutes	ELL, L1
	—— Meeting Special Needs, TWE, p. 760	25–35 minutes	L1
	—— Interdisciplinary Connections Activity, TWE, p. 761	20–30 minutes	L2
	—— Critical Thinking Activity, TWE, p. 762	20–25 minutes	L2
	—— Graphic Organizer Transparencies Strategies and Activities, TCR 🔖 📁	20–25 minutes	All levels
	Independent Practice		
	—— Guided Reading Activity 26–2, TCR 📁	15–20 minutes	ELL, L1
	ASSESS MENU **Evaluate**		
	—— Section Quiz 26–2, TCR 📁	10-15 minutes	All levels
	—— Interactive Tutor Self-Assessment CD-ROM ⊙	20–30 minutes	All levels
	—— ExamView® Pro Testmaker CD-ROM ⊙	15–20 minutes	All levels
	Reteach		
	—— Reteaching Activity 26–2, TCR 📁	15–20 minutes	ELL, L1
	—— Reading Essentials and Study Guide 26–2, TCR 📁	25–35 minutes	ELL, L1
	Enrich		
	—— Enrichment Activity 26–2, TCR 📁	10–15 minutes	L2, L3
	—— Primary Source Reading 26, TCR 📁	15–20 minutes	All levels
	CLOSE MENU		
	—— Close, TWE, p. 763	10–15 minutes	All levels

See Optional Resources menu on page viii.

On the Home Front

Section 3 (pp. 764–768)

LOCAL OBJECTIVES	TWE—Teacher Wraparound Edition TCR—Teacher Classroom Resources 📁 Blackline Master 🖋 Transparency 💿 CD-ROM 📀 DVD 📕 Poster 🎵 Music Program 🎧 Audio Program 📼 Videocassette 🔗 Internet Resources

	OBJECTIVES 1. Discuss what steps the United States took to prepare for fighting the war. 2. Explain how the war affected Americans.		
	FOCUS MENU	**SUGGESTED TIME RANGES**	**SUGGESTED LEVELS**
	—— Daily Focus Skills Transparency 26-3, TCR 🖋 📁	5–10 minutes	L1
	—— Preteaching Vocabulary, TWE, p. 764	5–10 minutes	All levels
	—— Audio Program Chapter 26 🎧	20–25 minutes	All levels
	TEACH MENU **Guided Practice**		
	—— Activity, TWE, p. 765	5–10 minutes	L1
	—— Cooperative Learning Activity, TWE, p. 765	40–60 minutes	L2
	—— Meeting Special Needs, TWE, p. 766	25–35 minutes	L1
	—— Interdisciplinary Connections Activity, TWE, p. 767	20–30 minutes	L2
	—— Graphic Organizer Transparencies Strategies and Activities, TCR 🖋 📁	20–25 minutes	All levels
	Independent Practice		
	—— Guided Reading Activity 26–3, TCR 📁	15–20 minutes	ELL, L1
	ASSESS MENU **Evaluate**		
	—— Section Quiz 26–3, TCR 📁	10–15 minutes	All levels
	—— Interactive Tutor Self-Assessment CD-ROM 💿	20–30 minutes	All levels
	—— ExamView® Pro Testmaker CD-ROM 💿	15–20 minutes	All levels
	Reteach		
	—— Reteaching Activity 26–3, TCR 📁	15–20 minutes	ELL, L1
	—— Reading Essentials and Study Guide 26–3, TCR 📁	25–35 minutes	ELL, L1
	Enrich		
	—— Enrichment Activity 26–3, TCR 📁	10–15 minutes	L2, L3
	—— Linking Past and Present Activity 26, TCR 📁	20–30 minutes	All levels
	CLOSE MENU		
	—— Close, TWE, p. 768	10–15 minutes	All levels

See Optional Resources menu on page viii.

Grade _____ Class(es) _____ Date _____ M Tu W Th F

Teacher's Name _____ Date _____

War in Europe and Africa
Section 4 (pp. 770–776)

LOCAL OBJECTIVES	TWE—Teacher Wraparound Edition TCR—Teacher Classroom Resources
	📁 Blackline Master 🏷 Transparency 💿 CD-ROM ⊙ DVD 📕 Poster
	🏴 Music Program 🔊 Audio Program 📼 Videocassette 🖱 Internet Resources

	OBJECTIVES		
	1. Identify the important battles that took place in North Africa, Italy, and the Soviet Union between 1942 and 1944.		
	2. Summarize the factors that contributed to the Allied victory in Europe.		

	FOCUS MENU	**SUGGESTED TIME RANGES**	**SUGGESTED LEVELS**
	____ Daily Focus Skills Transparency 26–4, TCR 🏷 📁	5–10 minutes	L1
	____ Preteaching Vocabulary, TWE, p. 770	5–10 minutes	All levels
	____ Audio Program Chapter 26 🔊	20–25 minutes	All levels

	TEACH MENU		
	Guided Practice		
	____ Activity, TWE, p. 771	5–10 minutes	L1
	____ Cooperative Learning Activity, TWE, p. 771	40–60 minutes	L2
	____ Meeting Special Needs, TWE, p. 772	25–35 minutes	L1
	____ Interdisciplinary Connections Activity, TWE, p. 773	20–30 minutes	L2
	____ Critical Thinking Activity, TWE, p. 774	20–25 minutes	L2
	____ Extending the Content, TWE, p. 775	5–10 minutes	All levels
	____ Graphic Organizer Transparencies Strategies and Activities, TCR 🏷 📁	20–25 minutes	All levels
	____ American Art and Architecture 🏷 📁	25–30 minutes	All levels
	____ Why It Matters Chapter Transparency Strategy and Activity 26, TCR 🏷 📁	25–30 minutes	All levels
	Independent Practice		
	____ Guided Reading Activity 26–4, TCR 📁	15–20 minutes	ELL, L1

	ASSESS MENU		
	Evaluate		
	____ Section Quiz 26–4, TCR 📁	10–15 minutes	All levels
	____ Interactive Tutor Self-Assessment CD-ROM 💿	20–30 minutes	All levels
	____ ExamView® Pro Testmaker CD-ROM 💿	15–20 minutes	All levels
	Reteach		
	____ Reteaching Activity 26–4, TCR 📁	15–20 minutes	ELL, L1
	____ Reading Essentials and Study Guide 26–4, TCR 📁	25–35 minutes	ELL, L1
	Enrich		
	____ Enrichment Activity 26–4, TCR 📁	10–15 minutes	L2, L3

	CLOSE MENU		
	____ Close, TWE, p. 776	10–15 minutes	All levels

See Optional Resources menu on page viii.

War in the Pacific

Section 5 (pp. 777–780)

LOCAL OBJECTIVES	TWE—Teacher Wraparound Edition TCR—Teacher Classroom Resources
	🗁 Blackline Master 🔥 Transparency 💿 CD-ROM 🔘 DVD 💻 Poster
	🎌 Music Program 🎧 Audio Program 📼 Videocassette ✒ Internet Resources

		SUGGESTED TIME RANGES	SUGGESTED LEVELS
	OBJECTIVES		
	1. Describe how the United States planned to gain control of the Pacific region.		
	2. Explain what role the atomic bomb played in ending the war.		
	FOCUS MENU		
	____ Daily Focus Skills Transparency 26–5, TCR 🔥 🗁	5–10 minutes	L1
	____ Vocabulary PuzzleMaker CD-ROM 💿	5–10 minutes	All levels
	____ Audio Program Chapter 26 🎧	20–25 minutes	All levels
	TEACH MENU		
	Guided Practice		
	____ Activity, TWE, p. 778	5–10 minutes	L1
	____ Cooperative Learning Activity, TWE, p. 778	40–60 minutes	ELL, L1
	____ Meeting Special Needs, TWE, p. 779	25–35 minutes	L1
	____ Graphic Organizer Transparency Strategy and Activity 26, TCR 🔥 🗁	15–20 minutes	L2
	Independent Practice		
	____ Guided Reading Activity 26–5 TCR 🗁	15–20 minutes	ELL, L1
	____ Vocabulary Activity 26, TCR 🗁	20–30 minutes	All levels
	____ Chapter Skills Activity 26, TCR 🗁	20–30 minutes	L1
	____ Critical Thinking Activity 26, TCR 🗁	20–30 minutes	L1
	____ Geography and History Activity 26, TCR 🗁	15–20 minutes	L1
	____ Time Line Activity 26, TCR 🗁	10–15 minutes	All levels
	ASSESS MENU		
	Evaluate		
	____ Section Quiz 26–5, TCR 🗁	10–15 minutes	All levels
	____ Performance Assessment Activity 26, TCR 🗁	25–30 minutes	All levels
	____ Interactive Tutor Self-Assessment CD-ROM 💿	20–30 minutes	All levels
	____ ExamView® Pro Testmaker CD-ROM 💿	15–20 minutes	All levels
	____ History Online Activity ✒	15–20 minutes	All levels
	Reteach		
	____ Reteaching Activity 26–5, TCR 🗁	15–20 minutes	ELL, L1
	____ Reading Essentials and Study Guide 26–5, TCR 🗁	25–25 minutes	ELL, L1
	____ Take-Home Review Activity 26, TCR 🗁	10–15 minutes	All levels
	____ MindJogger Videoquiz, Chapter 26 🔘 📼	20–25 minutes	All levels
	Enrich		
	____ Enrichment Activity 26–5, TCR 🗁	10–15 minutes	L2, L3
	CLOSE MENU		
	____ Close, TWE, p. 780	10–15 minutes	All levels

See Optional Resources menu on page viii.

Grade _____ Class(es) _____ Date _____ M Tu W Th F

Teacher's Name _____ Date _____

Cold War Origins
Section 1 *(pp. 788–794)*

LOCAL OBJECTIVES	TWE—Teacher Wraparound Edition TCR—Teacher Classroom Resources 📁 Blackline Master ✒ Transparency ⦿ CD-ROM ⦿ DVD 📕 Poster 🎵 Music Program 🔊 Audio Program 📼 Videocassette 🖱 Internet Resources

	OBJECTIVES **1.** Explain how the United States attempted to stop the spread of communism. **2.** Describe how foreign policy changed as a result of the Cold War.		
	FOCUS MENU	**SUGGESTED TIME RANGES**	**SUGGESTED LEVELS**
	____ Daily Focus Skills Transparency 27–1, TCR ✒ 📁	5–10 minutes	L1
	____ Preteaching Vocabulary, TWE, p. 788	5–10 minutes	All levels
	____ History Online Chapter 27 Overview 🖱	15–20 minutes	All levels
	____ Audio Program Chapter 27 🔊	20–25 minutes	All levels
	TEACH MENU **Guided Practice**		
	____ Time Line Activity, TWE, p. 787	5–10 minutes	All levels
	____ Activity, TWE, p. 789	5–10 minutes	L1
	____ Cooperative Learning Activity, TWE, p. 789	40–60 minutes	L2
	____ Meeting Special Needs, TWE, p. 790	25–35 minutes	L1
	____ Interdisciplinary Connections Activity, TWE, p. 791	20–30 minutes	L3
	____ Critical Thinking Activity, TWE, p. 792	20–25 minutes	L3
	____ Extending the Content, TWE, p. 793	5–10 minutes	All levels
	____ Graphic Organizer Transparencies Strategies and Activities, TCR ✒ 📁	20–25 minutes	All levels
	____ Why It Matters Chapter Transparency Strategy and Activity 27, TCR ✒ 📁	25–30 minutes	All levels
	Independent Practice		
	____ Guided Reading Activity 27–1, TCR 📁	15–20 minutes	ELL, L1
	____ Reading and Study Skills Foldable, p. 787	10–15 minutes	All levels
	ASSESS MENU **Evaluate**		
	____ Section Quiz 27–1, TCR 📁	10–15 minutes	All levels
	____ Interactive Tutor Self-Assessment CD-ROM ⦿	20–30 minutes	All levels
	____ ExamView® Pro Testmaker CD-ROM ⦿	15–20 minutes	All levels
	Reteach		
	____ Reteaching Activity 27–1, TCR 📁	15–20 minutes	ELL, L1
	____ Reading Essentials and Study Guide 27–1, TCR 📁	25–35 minutes	ELL, L1
	Enrich		
	____ Enrichment Activity 27–1, TCR 📁	10–15 minutes	L2, L3
	____ Primary Source Reading 27, TCR 📁	20–30 minutes	All levels
	CLOSE MENU		
	____ Close, TWE, p. 794	10–15 minutes	All levels

See Optional Resources menu on page viii.

The American Journey

Postwar Politics

Section 2 *(pp. 796–801)*

LOCAL OBJECTIVES	TWE—Teacher Wraparound Edition TCR—Teacher Classroom Resources 📁 Blackline Master 🕹 Transparency 💿 CD-ROM 💿 DVD 🖼 Poster 🎵 Music Program 🎧 Audio Program 📼 Videocassette 🖱 Internet Resources

<table>
<tr><td></td><td colspan="3">

OBJECTIVES

1. Review the economic problems Americans faced after World War II.

2. Discuss how President Truman and Congress proposed to deal with the nation's problems.
</td></tr>
<tr><td></td><td>**FOCUS MENU**</td><td>**SUGGESTED TIME RANGES**</td><td>**SUGGESTED LEVELS**</td></tr>
<tr><td></td><td>—— Daily Focus Skills Transparency 27–2, TCR 🕹 📁</td><td>5–10 minutes</td><td>L1</td></tr>
<tr><td></td><td>—— Preteaching Vocabulary, TWE, p. 796</td><td>5–10 minutes</td><td>All levels</td></tr>
<tr><td></td><td>—— Audio Program Chapter 27 🎧</td><td>20–25 minutes</td><td>All levels</td></tr>
<tr><td></td><td>

TEACH MENU

Guided Practice
</td><td></td><td></td></tr>
<tr><td></td><td>—— Activity, TWE, p. 797</td><td>5–10 minutes</td><td>L2</td></tr>
<tr><td></td><td>—— Cooperative Learning Activity, TWE, p. 797</td><td>40–60 minutes</td><td>L2</td></tr>
<tr><td></td><td>—— Meeting Special Needs, TWE, p. 798</td><td>25–35 minutes</td><td>L1</td></tr>
<tr><td></td><td>—— Interdisciplinary Connections Activity, TWE, p. 799</td><td>20–30 minutes</td><td>L2</td></tr>
<tr><td></td><td>—— Critical Thinking Activity, TWE, p. 800</td><td>20–25 minutes</td><td>L2</td></tr>
<tr><td></td><td>—— Graphic Organizer Transparencies
 Strategies and Activities, TCR 🕹 📁</td><td>20–25 minutes</td><td>All levels</td></tr>
<tr><td></td><td>**Independent Practice**</td><td></td><td></td></tr>
<tr><td></td><td>—— Guided Reading Activity 27–2, TCR 📁</td><td>15–20 minutes</td><td>ELL, L1</td></tr>
<tr><td></td><td>

ASSESS MENU

Evaluate
</td><td></td><td></td></tr>
<tr><td></td><td>—— Section Quiz 27–2, TCR 📁</td><td>10–15 minutes</td><td>All levels</td></tr>
<tr><td></td><td>—— Interactive Tutor Self-Assessment CD-ROM 💿</td><td>20–30 minutes</td><td>All levels</td></tr>
<tr><td></td><td>—— ExamView® Pro Testmaker CD-ROM 💿</td><td>15–20 minutes</td><td>All levels</td></tr>
<tr><td></td><td>**Reteach**</td><td></td><td></td></tr>
<tr><td></td><td>—— Reteaching Activity 27–2, TCR 📁</td><td>15–20 minutes</td><td>ELL, L1</td></tr>
<tr><td></td><td>—— Reading Essentials and Study Guide 27–2, TCR 📁</td><td>25–35 minutes</td><td>ELL, L1</td></tr>
<tr><td></td><td>**Enrich**</td><td></td><td></td></tr>
<tr><td></td><td>—— Enrichment Activity 27–2, TCR 📁</td><td>10–15 minutes</td><td>L2, L3</td></tr>
<tr><td></td><td>—— Linking Past and Present Activity 27, TCR 📁</td><td>15–20 minutes</td><td>All levels</td></tr>
<tr><td></td><td>

CLOSE MENU

—— Close, TWE, p. 801
</td><td>10–15 minutes</td><td>All levels</td></tr>
</table>

See Optional Resources menu on page viii.

The Korean War

Section 3 *(pp. 802–805)*

LOCAL OBJECTIVES	TWE—Teacher Wraparound Edition	TCR—Teacher Classroom Resources

Blackline Master Transparency CD-ROM DVD Poster
Music Program Audio Program Videocassette Internet Resources

OBJECTIVES

1. Cite the events that led to the Korean War.

2. Explain how America's war aims changed during the war.

FOCUS MENU	SUGGESTED TIME RANGES	SUGGESTED LEVELS
—— Daily Focus Skills Transparency 27–3, TCR	5–10 minutes	L1
—— Preteaching Vocabulary, TWE, p. 802	5–10 minutes	All levels
—— Audio Program Chapter 27	20–25 minutes	All levels

TEACH MENU

Guided Practice

—— Activity, TWE, p. 803	5–10 minutes	L1
—— Cooperative Learning Activity, TWE, p. 803	40–60 minutes	L2
—— Meeting Special Needs, TWE, p. 804	25–35 minutes	L1
—— Graphic Organizer Transparency Strategy and Activity 27, TCR	15–20 minutes	L2

Independent Practice

—— Guided Reading Activity 27–3, TCR	15–20 minutes	ELL, L1

ASSESS MENU

Evaluate

—— Section Quiz 27–3, TCR	10–15 minutes	All levels
—— Interactive Tutor Self-Assessment CD-ROM	20–30 minutes	All levels
—— ExamView® Pro Testmaker CD-ROM	15–20 minutes	All levels
—— History Online Activity	15–20 minutes	All levels

Reteach

—— Reteaching Activity 27–3, TCR	15–20 minutes	ELL, L1
—— Reading Essentials and Study Guide 27–3, TCR	25–35 minutes	ELL, L1

Enrich

—— Enrichment Activity 27–3, TCR	10–15 minutes	L2, L3

CLOSE MENU

—— Close, TWE, p. 805	10–15 minutes	All levels

See Optional Resources menu on page viii.

The Red Scare

Section 4 *(pp. 806–809)*

LOCAL OBJECTIVES	TWE—Teacher Wraparound Edition TCR—Teacher Classroom Resources
	🗂 Blackline Master ⚱ Transparency ◉ CD-ROM ◉ DVD ▭ Poster
	🎵 Music Program ◉ Audio Program ▦ Videocassette ⬳ Internet Resources

OBJECTIVES

1. Identify the effects that Cold-War fears had on domestic politics.

2. Describe how McCarthyism affected the nation.

		SUGGESTED TIME RANGES	SUGGESTED LEVELS
FOCUS MENU			
—— Daily Focus Skills Transparency 27–4, TCR ⚱ 🗂		5–10 minutes	L1
—— Vocabulary PuzzleMaker CD-ROM ◉		5–10 minutes	All levels
—— Audio Program Chapter 27 ◉		20–25 minutes	All levels
TEACH MENU			
Guided Practice			
—— Activity, TWE, p. 807		5–10 minutes	ELL, L1
—— Cooperative Learning Activity, TWE, p. 807		40–60 minutes	L2
—— Meeting Special Needs, TWE, p. 808		25–35 minutes	L1
—— Graphic Organizer Transparencies Strategies and Activities, TCR ⚱ 🗂		20–25 minutes	All levels
Independent Practice			
—— Guided Reading Activity 27–4 TCR 🗂		15–20 minutes	ELL, L1
—— Vocabulary Activity 27, TCR 🗂		20–30 minutes	All levels
—— Chapter Skills Activity 27, TCR 🗂		40–60 minutes	L2, L3
—— Critical Thinking Activity 27, TCR 🗂		15–20 minutes	L1
—— Geography and History Activity 27, TCR 🗂		15–20 minutes	All levels
—— Time Line Activity 27, TCR 🗂		15–20 minutes	All levels
ASSESS MENU			
Evaluate			
—— Section Quiz 27–4, TCR 🗂		10–15 minutes	All levels
—— Performance Assessment Activity 27, TCR 🗂		25–30 minutes	All levels
—— Interactive Tutor Self-Assessment CD-ROM ◉		20–30 minutes	All levels
—— ExamView® Pro Testmaker CD-ROM ◉		15–20 minutes	All levels
Reteach			
—— Reteaching Activity 27–4, TCR 🗂		15–20 minutes	ELL, L1
—— Reading Essentials and Study Guide 27–4, TCR 🗂		25–35 minutes	ELL, L1
—— Take-Home Review Activity 27, TCR 🗂		10–15 minutes	All levels
—— MindJogger Videoquiz, Chapter 27 ◉ ▦		20–25 minutes	All levels
Enrich			
—— Enrichment Activity 27–4, TCR 🗂		10–15 minutes	L2, L3
CLOSE MENU			
—— Close, TWE, p. 809		10–15 minutes	All levels

See Optional Resources menu on page viii.

Grade _____ Class(es) _____ Date _____ M Tu W Th F

Teacher's Name _____ Date _____

Eisenhower in the White House   Section 1 (pp. 814–820)

LOCAL OBJECTIVES	TWE—Teacher Wraparound Edition · TCR—Teacher Classroom Resources · Blackline Master · Transparency · CD-ROM · DVD · Poster · Music Program · Audio Program · Videocassette · Internet Resources		

OBJECTIVES

1. Describe the beliefs and policies that characterized the Eisenhower presidency.

2. Identify foreign policy challenges that the Eisenhower administration faced.

FOCUS MENU	SUGGESTED TIME RANGES	SUGGESTED LEVELS
—— Daily Focus Skills Transparency 28–1, TCR	5–10 minutes	L1
—— Preteaching Vocabulary, TWE, p. 814	5–10 minutes	All levels
—— History Online Chapter 28 Overview	15–20 minutes	All levels
—— Audio Program Chapter 28	20–25 minutes	All levels

TEACH MENU

Guided Practice

	SUGGESTED TIME RANGES	SUGGESTED LEVELS
—— Time Line Activity, TWE, p. 813	5–10 minutes	All levels
—— Activity, TWE, p. 815	5–10 minutes	L1
—— Cooperative Learning Activity, TWE, p. 815	40–60 minutes	L2
—— Meeting Special Needs, TWE, p. 816	25–35 minutes	L1
—— Interdisciplinary Connections Activity, TWE, p. 817	20–30 minutes	L3
—— Critical Thinking Activity, TWE, p. 818	20–25 minutes	L3
—— Extending the Content, TWE, p. 819	5–10 minutes	All levels
—— Graphic Organizer Transparencies Strategies and Activities, TCR	20–25 minutes	All levels

Independent Practice

—— Guided Reading Activity 28–1, TCR	15–20 minutes	ELL, L1
—— Reading and Study Skills Foldable, p. 813	10–15 minutes	All levels

ASSESS MENU

Evaluate

—— Section Quiz 28–1, TCR	10–15 minutes	All levels
—— Interactive Tutor Self-Assessment CD-ROM	20–30 minutes	All levels
—— ExamView® Pro Testmaker CD-ROM	15–20 minutes	All levels

Reteach

—— Reteaching Activity 28–1, TCR	15–20 minutes	ELL, L1
—— Reading Essentials and Study Guide 28–1, TCR	25–35 minutes	ELL, L1

Enrich

—— Enrichment Activity 28–1, TCR	10–15 minutes	L2, L3
—— Linking Past and Present Activity 28, TCR	15–20 minutes	All levels

CLOSE MENU

—— Close, TWE, p. 820	10–15 minutes	All levels

See Optional Resources menu on page viii.

1950s Prosperity

Section 2 *(pp. 821–826)*

LOCAL OBJECTIVES	TWE—Teacher Wraparound Edition TCR—Teacher Classroom Resources
	📁 Blackline Master 🔦 Transparency 💿 CD-ROM 💿 DVD 📗 Poster
	🎵 Music Program 🎧 Audio Program 📼 Videocassette 🖱 Internet Resources

	OBJECTIVES		
	1. List the factors that helped the economy grow during the 1950s.		
	2. Describe the effects of the era's prosperity on American society and culture.		

	FOCUS MENU	**SUGGESTED TIME RANGES**	**SUGGESTED LEVELS**
	—— Daily Focus Skills Transparency 28–2, TCR 🔦 📁	5–10 minutes	L1
	—— Preteaching Vocabulary, TWE, p. 821	5–10 minutes	All levels
	—— Audio Program Chapter 28 🎧	20–25 minutes	All levels

	TEACH MENU		
	Guided Practice		
	—— Activity, TWE, p. 822	5-10 minutes	L1
	—— Cooperative Learning Activity, TWE, p. 822	40–60 minutes	L1
	—— Meeting Special Needs, TWE, p. 823	25–35 minutes	L1
	—— Interdisciplinary Connections Activity, TWE, p. 824	20–30 minutes	L2
	—— Critical Thinking Activity, TWE, p. 825	20–25 minutes	L2
	—— Graphic Organizer Transparency Strategy and Activity 28, TCR 🔦 📁	15–20 minutes	L2
	Independent Practice		
	—— Guided Reading Activity 28–2, TCR 📁	15–20 minutes	ELL, L1

	ASSESS MENU		
	Evaluate		
	—— Section Quiz 28–2, TCR 📁	10–15 minutes	All levels
	—— Interactive Tutor Self-Assessment CD-ROM 💿	20–30 minutes	All levels
	—— ExamView® Pro Testmaker CD-ROM 💿	15–20 minutes	All levels
	Reteach		
	—— Reteaching Activity 28–2, TCR 📁	15–20 minutes	ELL, L1
	—— Reading Essentials and Study Guide 28–2, TCR 📁	25–35 minutes	ELL, L1
	Enrich		
	—— Enrichment Activity 28–2, TCR 📁	10–15 minutes	L2, L3
	—— Primary Source Reading 28, TCR 📁	20–30 minutes	All levels

	CLOSE MENU		
	—— Close, TWE, p. 826	10–15 minutes	All levels

See Optional Resources menu on page viii.

Problems in a Time of Plenty Section 3 *(pp. 828–831)*

LOCAL OBJECTIVES	TWE—Teacher Wraparound Edition TCR—Teacher Classroom Resources 📁 Blackline Master 🖌 Transparency 💿 CD-ROM 💿 DVD 📖 Poster 🎵 Music Program 🔊 Audio Program 📺 Videocassette 🖱 Internet Resources

	OBJECTIVES **1.** Identify the groups that did not share in the prosperity of the 1950s. **2.** Explain why some people criticized American values of the period.		

	FOCUS MENU	**SUGGESTED TIME RANGES**	**SUGGESTED LEVELS**
	—— Daily Focus Skills Transparency 28–3, TCR 🖌 📁	5–10 minutes	L1
	—— Vocabulary PuzzleMaker CD-ROM 💿	5–10 minutes	All levels
	—— Audio Program Chapter 28 🔊	20–25 minutes	All levels

	TEACH MENU		
	Guided Practice		
	—— Activity, TWE, p. 829	5–10 minutes	L2
	—— Cooperative Learning Activity, TWE, p. 829	40–60 minutes	L2
	—— Meeting Special Needs, TWE, p. 830	25–35 minutes	L1
	—— Graphic Organizer Transparencies Strategies and Activities, TCR 🖌 📁	20–25 minutes	All levels
	—— Why It Matters Chapter Transparency Strategy and Activity 28, TCR 🖌 📁	25–30 minutes	All levels
	Independent Practice		
	—— Guided Reading Activity 28–3 TCR 📁	15–20 minutes	ELL, L1
	—— Vocabulary Activity 28, TCR 📁	20–30 minutes	All levels
	—— Chapter Skills Activity 28, TCR 📁	20–30 minutes	All levels
	—— Critical Thinking Activity 28, TCR 📁	20–30 minutes	L1
	—— Geography and History Activity 28, TCR 📁	15–20 minutes	All levels
	—— Time Line Activity 28, TCR 📁	15–20 minutes	All levels

	ASSESS MENU		
	Evaluate		
	—— Section Quiz 28–3, TCR 📁	10–15 minutes	All levels
	—— Performance Assessment Activity 28, TCR 📁	00–00 minutes	Need levels
	—— Interactive Tutor Self-Assessment CD-ROM 💿	20–30 minutes	All levels
	—— ExamView® Pro Testmaker CD-ROM 💿	15–20 minutes	All levels
	—— History Online Activity 🖱	15–20 minutes	All levels
	Reteach		
	—— Reteaching Activity 28–3, TCR 📁	15–20 minutes	ELL, L1
	—— Reading Essentials and Study Guide 28–3, TCR 📁	25–35 minutes	ELL, L1
	—— Take-Home Review Activity 28, TCR 📁	00–00 minutes	Need levels
	—— MindJogger Videoquiz, Chapter 28 💿 📺	00–00 minutes	Need levels
	Enrich		
	—— Enrichment Activity 28–3, TCR 📁	10–15 minutes	L2, L3

	CLOSE MENU		
	—— Close, TWE, p. 831	10–15 minutes	All levels

See Optional Resources menu on page viii.

The Civil Rights Movement Section 1 *(pp. 838–842)*

LOCAL OBJECTIVES	TWE—Teacher Wraparound Edition TCR—Teacher Classroom Resources 📁 Blackline Master ⚖ Transparency 💿 CD-ROM 📀 DVD 📕 Poster 🎵 Music Program 🎧 Audio Program 📼 Videocassette ⌁ Internet Resources

OBJECTIVES

1. Understand how a Supreme Court decision helped African Americans in their struggle for equal rights.

2. Explain why Martin Luther King, Jr., emerged as a leader.

FOCUS MENU	SUGGESTED TIME RANGES	SUGGESTED LEVELS
—— Daily Focus Skills Transparency 29–1, TCR ⚖ 📁	5–10 minutes	L1
—— Preteaching Vocabulary, TWE, p. 838	5–10 minutes	All levels
—— History Online Chapter 29 Overview ⌁	15–20 minutes	All levels
—— Audio Program Chapter 29 🎧	20–25 minutes	All levels

TEACH MENU

Guided Practice

—— Time Line Activity, TWE, p. 837	10–15 minutes	All levels
—— Cooperative Learning Activity, TWE, p. 839	40–60 minutes	L1
—— Meeting Special Needs, TWE, p. 840	25–35 minutes	L1
—— Interdisciplinary Connections Activity, TWE, p. 841	20–30 minutes	L2
—— Graphic Organizer Transparencies Strategies and Activities, TCR ⚖ 📁	20–25 minutes	All levels

Independent Practice

—— Guided Reading Activity 29–1, TCR 📁	15–20 minutes	ELL, L1
—— Reading and Study Skills Foldable, p. 837	10–15 minutes	All levels

ASSESS MENU

Evaluate

—— Section Quiz 29–1, TCR 📁	10–15 minutes	All levels
—— Interactive Tutor Self-Assessment CD-ROM 💿	20–30 minutes	All levels
—— ExamView® Pro Testmaker CD-ROM 💿	15–20 minutes	All levels

Reteach

—— Reteaching Activity 29–1, TCR 📁	15–20 minutes	ELL, L1
—— Reading Essentials and Study Guide 29–1, TCR 📁	25–35 minutes	ELL, L1

Enrich

—— Enrichment Activity 29–1, TCR 📁	10–15 minutes	L2, L3
—— Primary Source Reading 29, TCR 📁	20–30 minutes	All levels

CLOSE MENU

—— Close, TWE, p. 842	10–15 minutes	All levels

See Optional Resources menu on page viii.

Kennedy and Johnson

Section 2 *(pp. 844–847)*

LOCAL OBJECTIVES	TWE—Teacher Wraparound Edition TCR—Teacher Classroom Resources
	📁 Blackline Master 🕹 Transparency 💿 CD-ROM 💿 DVD 📕 Poster
	🎵 Music Program 🎧 Audio Program 📼 Videocassette 🖱 Internet Resources

		SUGGESTED TIME RANGES	SUGGESTED LEVELS
	OBJECTIVES		
	1. Identify the goals for Kennedy's New Frontier.		
	2. Describe what new programs were created as part of the Great Society.		
	FOCUS MENU		
	—— Daily Focus Skills Transparency 29–2, TCR 🕹 📁	5–10 minutes	L1
	—— Preteaching Vocabulary, TWE, p. 844	5–10 minutes	All levels
	—— Audio Program Chapter 29 🎧	20–25 minutes	All levels
	TEACH MENU		
	Guided Practice		
	—— Activity, TWE, p. 845	5–10 minutes	ELL, L1
	—— Cooperative Learning Activity, TWE, p. 845	40–60 minutes	L2
	—— Meeting Special Needs, TWE, p. 846	25–35 minutes	L1
	—— Graphic Organizer Transparencies Strategies and Activities, TCR 🕹 📁	20–25 minutes	All levels
	Independent Practice		
	—— Guided Reading Activity 29–2, TCR 📁	15–20 minutes	ELL, L1
	ASSESS MENU		
	Evaluate		
	—— Section Quiz 29–2, TCR 📁	10–15 minutes	All levels
	—— Interactive Tutor Self-Assessment CD-ROM 💿	20–30 minutes	All levels
	—— ExamView® Pro Testmaker CD-ROM 💿	15–20 minutes	All levels
	Reteach		
	—— Reteaching Activity 29–2, TCR 📁	15–20 minutes	ELL, L1
	—— Reading Essentials and Study Guide 29–2, TCR 📁	25–35 minutes	ELL, L1
	Enrich		
	—— Enrichment Activity 29–2, TCR 📁	10–15 minutes	L2, L3
	CLOSE MENU		
	—— Close, TWE, p. 847	10–15 minutes	All levels

See Optional Resources menu on page viii.

The Struggle Continues Section 3 *(pp. 848–853)*

LOCAL OBJECTIVES	TWE—Teacher Wraparound Edition TCR—Teacher Classroom Resources 🗂 Blackline Master ✋ Transparency 💿 CD-ROM 💿 DVD 📕 Poster 🎵 Music Program 🔊 Audio Program 📼 Videocassette ✏ Internet Resources		
	OBJECTIVES **1.** Cite what actions African Americans took in the early 1960s to secure their rights. **2.** Understand how tensions erupted in violence in many American cities.		
	FOCUS MENU	**SUGGESTED TIME RANGES**	**SUGGESTED LEVELS**
	—— Daily Focus Skills Transparency 29–3, TCR ✋ 🗂	5–10 minutes	L1
	—— Preteaching Vocabulary, TWE, p. 848	5–10 minutes	All levels
	—— Audio Program Chapter 29 🔊	20–25 minutes	All levels
	TEACH MENU **Guided Practice**		
	—— Activity, TWE, p. 849	5–10 minutes	ELL, L1
	—— Cooperative Learning Activity, TWE, p. 849	40–60 minutes	L2
	—— Meeting Special Needs, TWE, p. 850	25–35 minutes	L1
	—— Interdisciplinary Connections Activity, TWE, p. 851	20–30 minutes	L2
	—— Critical Thinking Activity, TWE, p. 852	20–25 minutes	L2
	—— Graphic Organizer Transparencies Strategies and Activities, TCR ✋ 🗂	20–25 minutes	All levels
	Independent Practice		
	—— Guided Reading Activity 29–3, TCR 🗂	15–20 minutes	ELL, L1
	ASSESS MENU **Evaluate**		
	—— Section Quiz 29–3, TCR 🗂	10–15 minutes	All levels
	—— Interactive Tutor Self-Assessment CD-ROM 💿	20–30 minutes	All levels
	—— ExamView® Pro Testmaker CD-ROM 💿	15–20 minutes	All levels
	Reteach		
	—— Reteaching Activity 29–3, TCR 🗂	15–20 minutes	ELL, L1
	—— Reading Essentials and Study Guide 29–3, TCR 🗂	25–35 minutes	ELL, L1
	Enrich		
	—— Enrichment Activity 29–3, TCR 🗂	10–15 minutes	L2, L3
	—— Linking Past and Present Activity 29, TCR 🗂	15–20 minutes	All levels
	CLOSE MENU		
	—— Close, TWE, p. 853	10–15 minutes	All levels

See Optional Resources menu on page viii.

Grade _____ Class(es) _____ Date _____ M Tu W Th F

Teacher's Name _____ Date _____

Other Groups Seek Rights

Section 4 *(pp. 856–860)*

LOCAL OBJECTIVES	TWE—Teacher Wraparound Edition TCR—Teacher Classroom Resources
	📁 Blackline Master 🖋 Transparency ◉ CD-ROM ◉ DVD 📱 Poster
	🎌 Music Program 🎧 Audio Program 📼 Videocassette ✒ Internet Resources

OBJECTIVES

1. Examine the steps women and minorities took to improve their lives.
2. Identify the new leaders that emerged.

FOCUS MENU	SUGGESTED TIME RANGES	SUGGESTED LEVELS
—— Daily Focus Skills Transparency 29–4, TCR 🖋 📁	5–10 minutes	L1
—— Vocabulary PuzzleMaker CD-ROM ◉	5–10 minutes	All levels
—— Audio Program Chapter 29 🎧	20–25 minutes	All levels

TEACH MENU

Guided Practice

—— Activity, TWE, p. 857	5–10 minutes	L2
—— Cooperative Learning Activity, TWE, p. 857	40–60 minutes	L2
—— Meeting Special Needs, TWE, p. 858	25–35 minutes	L1
—— Interdisciplinary Connections Activity, TWE, p. 859	20–30 minutes	L3
—— Graphic Organizer Transparency Strategy and Activity 29, TCR 🖋 📁	15–20 minutes	L2
—— Why It Matters Chapter Transparency Strategy and Activity 29, TCR 🖋 📁	25–30 minutes	All levels

Independent Practice

—— Guided Reading Activity 29–4 TCR 📁	15–20 minutes	ELL, L1
—— Vocabulary Activity 29, TCR 📁	20–30 minutes	All levels
—— Chapter Skills Activity 29, TCR 📁	10–15 minutes	L1
—— Critical Thinking Activity 29, TCR 📁	15–20 minutes	L1
—— Geography and History Activity 29, TCR 📁	10–15 minutes	All levels
—— Time Line Activity 29, TCR 📁	15–20 minutes	All levels

ASSESS MENU

Evaluate

—— Section Quiz 29–4, TCR 📁	10–15 minutes	All levels
—— Performance Assessment Activity 29, TCR 📁	25–30 minutes	All levels
—— Interactive Tutor Self-Assessment CD-ROM ◉	20–30 minutes	All levels
—— ExamView® Pro Testmaker CD-ROM ◉	15–20 minutes	All levels
—— History Online Activity ✒	15–20 minutes	All levels

Reteach

—— Reteaching Activity 29–4, TCR 📁	15–20 minutes	ELL, L1
—— Reading Essentials and Study Guide 29–4, TCR 📁	25–35 minutes	ELL, L1
—— Take-Home Review Activity 29, TCR 📁	10–15 minutes	All levels
—— MindJogger Videoquiz, Chapter 29 ◉ 📼	20–25 minutes	All levels

Enrich

—— Enrichment Activity 29–4, TCR 📁	10–15 minutes	L2, L3

CLOSE MENU

—— Close, TWE, p. 860	10–15 minutes	All levels

See Optional Resources menu on page viii.

Kennedy's Foreign Policy   Section 1 *(pp. 866–870)*

LOCAL OBJECTIVES	TWE—Teacher Wraparound Edition TCR—Teacher Classroom Resources
	📁 Blackline Master 🖊 Transparency 💿 CD-ROM 💿 DVD 📋 Poster
	🎌 Music Program 🎧 Audio Program 📼 Videocassette 💻 Internet Resources

	OBJECTIVES		
	1. Understand how the Kennedy administration handled challenges to foreign affairs.		
	2. Explore what happened during the Cuban missile crisis.		
	FOCUS MENU	**SUGGESTED TIME RANGES**	**SUGGESTED LEVELS**
	____ Daily Focus Skills Transparency 30–1, TCR 🖊 📁	5–10 minutes	L1
	____ Preteaching Vocabulary, TWE, p. 866	5–10 minutes	All levels
	____ History Online Chapter 30 Overview 💻	15–20 minutes	All levels
	____ Audio Program Chapter 30 🎧	20–25 minutes	All levels
	TEACH MENU		
	Guided Practice		
	____ Time Line Activity, TWE, p. 865	10–15 minutes	All levels
	____ Activity, TWE, p. 867	5–10 minutes	ELL, L1
	____ Cooperative Learning Activity, TWE, p. 867	40–60 minutes	L2
	____ Meeting Special Needs, TWE, p. 868	25–35 minutes	L1
	____ Interdisciplinary Connections Activity, TWE, p. 869	20–30 minutes	L2
	____ Graphic Organizer Transparencies Strategies and Activities, TCR 🖊 📁	20–25 minutes	All levels
	Independent Practice		
	____ Guided Reading Activity 30–1, TCR 📁	15–20 minutes	ELL, L1
	____ Reading and Study Skills Foldable, p. 865	10–15 minutes	All levels
	ASSESS MENU		
	Evaluate		
	____ Section Quiz 30–1, TCR 📁	10–15 minutes	All levels
	____ Interactive Tutor Self-Assessment CD-ROM 💿	20–30 minutes	All levels
	____ ExamView® Pro Testmaker CD-ROM 💿	15–20 minutes	All levels
	Reteach		
	____ Reteaching Activity 30–1, TCR 📁	15–20 minutes	ELL, L1
	____ Reading Essentials and Study Guide 30–1, TCR 📁	25–35 minutes	ELL, L1
	Enrich		
	____ Enrichment Activity 30–1, TCR 📁	10–15 minutes	L2, L3
	CLOSE MENU		
	____ Close, TWE, p. 870	10–15 minutes	All levels

See Optional Resources menu on page viii.

Grade _____ Class(es) _____ Date _____ M Tu W Th F

Teacher's Name _____ Date _____

War in Vietnam

Section 2 *(pp. 871–876)*

LOCAL OBJECTIVES	TWE—Teacher Wraparound Edition TCR—Teacher Classroom Resources 📁 Blackline Master ⚒ Transparency 💿 CD-ROM 💿 DVD 📕 Poster 🎵 Music Program 🔊 Audio Program 📼 Videocassette ✒ Internet Resources		
	OBJECTIVES **1.** Determine how Vietnam became a divided country. **2.** Understand why America increased its involvement in the Vietnam War.		
	FOCUS MENU	**SUGGESTED TIME RANGES**	**SUGGESTED LEVELS**
	—— Daily Focus Skills Transparency 30–2, TCR ⚒ 📁	5–10 minutes	L1
	—— Preteaching Vocabulary, TWE, p. 871	5–10 minutes	All levels
	—— Audio Program Chapter 30 🔊	20–25 minutes	All levels
	TEACH MENU **Guided Practice**		
	—— Activity, TWE, p. 872	5–10 minutes	L1
	—— Cooperative Learning Activity, TWE, p. 872	40–60 minutes	L2
	—— Meeting Special Needs, TWE, p. 873	25–35 minutes	L1
	—— Interdisciplinary Connections Activity, TWE, p. 874	20–30 minutes	L3
	—— Critical Thinking Activity, TWE, p. 875	20–25 minutes	L2
	—— Graphic Organizer Transparencies Strategies and Activities, TCR ⚒ 📁	20–25 minutes	All levels
	Independent Practice		
	—— Guided Reading Activity 30–2, TCR 📁	15–20 minutes	ELL, L1
	ASSESS MENU **Evaluate**		
	—— Section Quiz 30–2, TCR 📁	10–15 minutes	All levels
	—— Interactive Tutor Self-Assessment CD-ROM 💿	20–30 minutes	All levels
	—— ExamView® Pro Testmaker CD-ROM 💿	15–20 minutes	All levels
	Reteach		
	—— Reteaching Activity 30–2, TCR 📁	15–20 minutes	ELL, L1
	—— Reading Essentials and Study Guide 30–2, TCR 📁	25–35 minutes	ELL, L1
	Enrich		
	—— Enrichment Activity 30–2, TCR 📁	10–15 minutes	L2, L3
	—— Primary Source Reading 30, TCR 📁	20–30 minutes	All levels
	CLOSE MENU		
	—— Close, TWE, p. 876	10–15 minutes	All levels

See Optional Resources menu on page viii.

Grade _____ Class(es) _____ Date _____ M Tu W Th F

Teacher's Name _____ Date _____

The Vietnam Years at Home   Section 3 *(pp. 877–882)*

LOCAL OBJECTIVES	TWE—Teacher Wraparound Edition TCR—Teacher Classroom Resources 📁 Blackline Master ✋ Transparency ⊙ CD-ROM ⊙ DVD 📱 Poster 🏴 Music Program 🎧 Audio Program 📼 Videocassette 🖱 Internet Resources

OBJECTIVES
1. Describe what factors contributed to the rise of the protest movement.
2. Explain how Americans at home responded to the war in Vietnam.

FOCUS MENU	SUGGESTED TIME RANGES	SUGGESTED LEVELS
____ Daily Focus Skills Transparency 30–3, TCR ✋ 📁	5–10 minutes	L1
____ Preteaching Vocabulary, TWE, p. 877	5–10 minutes	All levels
____ Audio Program Chapter 30 🎧	20–25 minutes	All levels

TEACH MENU
Guided Practice

____ Activity, TWE, p. 878	5–10 minutes	L1
____ Cooperative Learning Activity, TWE, p. 878	40–60 minutes	L2
____ Meeting Special Needs, TWE, p. 879	25–35 minutes	L1
____ Interdisciplinary Connections Activity, TWE, p. 880	20–30 minutes	L2
____ Critical Thinking Activity, TWE, p. 881	20–25 minutes	L3
____ Graphic Organizer Transparency Strategy and Activity 30, TCR ✋ 📁	15–20 minutes	L2
____ Why It Matters Chapter Transparency Strategy and Activity 30, TCR ✋ 📁	25–30 minutes	All levels

Independent Practice

____ Guided Reading Activity 30–3, TCR 📁	15–20 minutes	ELL, L1

ASSESS MENU
Evaluate

____ Section Quiz 30–3, TCR 📁	10–15 minutes	All levels
____ Interactive Tutor Self-Assessment CD-ROM ⊙	20–30 minutes	All levels
____ ExamView® Pro Testmaker CD-ROM ⊙	15–20 minutes	All levels

Reteach

____ Reteaching Activity 30–3, TCR 📁	15–20 minutes	ELL, L1
____ Reading Essentials and Study Guide 30–3, TCR 📁	25–35 minutes	ELL, L1

Enrich

____ Enrichment Activity 30–3, TCR 📁	10–15 minutes	L2, L3
____ Linking Past and Present Activity 30, TCR 📁	15–20 minutes	All levels

CLOSE MENU

____ Close, TWE, p. 882	10–15 minutes	All levels

See Optional Resources menu on page viii.

Nixon and Vietnam

Section 4 (pp. 884–889)

LOCAL OBJECTIVES	TWE—Teacher Wraparound Edition TCR—Teacher Classroom Resources
	📁 Blackline Master ✋ Transparency 💿 CD-ROM 💿 DVD 📕 Poster
	🎵 Music Program 🎧 Audio Program 📼 Videocassette 🖱 Internet Resources

	OBJECTIVES		
	1. Explain the steps Nixon took to end the war in Vietnam.		
	2. Understand the various costs of the Vietnam War.		
	FOCUS MENU	**SUGGESTED TIME RANGES**	**SUGGESTED LEVELS**
	—— Daily Focus Skills Transparency 30–4, TCR ✋ 📁	5–10 minutes	L1
	—— Vocabulary PuzzleMaker CD-ROM 💿	5–10 minutes	All levels
	—— Audio Program Chapter 30 🎧	20–25 minutes	All levels
	TEACH MENU		
	Guided Practice		
	—— Activity, TWE, p. 885	5–10 minutes	L1
	—— Cooperative Learning Activity, TWE, p. 885	40–60 minutes	L2
	—— Meeting Special Needs, TWE, p. 886	25–35 minutes	L1
	—— Interdisciplinary Connections Activity, TWE, p. 887	20–30 minutes	ELL, L1
	—— Critical Thinking Activity, TWE, p. 888	20–25 minutes	L2
	—— Graphic Organizer Transparencies Strategies and Activities, TCR ✋ 📁	20–25 minutes	All levels
	Independent Practice		
	—— Guided Reading Activity 30–4 TCR 📁	15–20 minutes	ELL, L1
	—— Vocabulary Activity 30, TCR 📁	20–30 minutes	All levels
	—— Chapter Skills Activity 30, TCR 📁	30–40 minutes	L1
	—— Critical Thinking Activity 30, TCR 📁	15–20 minutes	L2
	—— Geography and History Activity 30, TCR 📁	10–15 minutes	All levels
	—— Time Line Activity 30, TCR 📁	15–20 minutes	All levels
	ASSESS MENU		
	Evaluate		
	—— Section Quiz 30–4, TCR 📁	10–15 minutes	All levels
	—— Performance Assessment Activity 30, TCR 📁	25–30 minutes	All levels
	—— Interactive Tutor Self-Assessment CD-ROM 💿	20–30 minutes	All levels
	—— ExamView® Pro Testmaker CD-ROM 💿	15–20 minutes	All levels
	—— History Online Activity 🖱	15–20 minutes	All levels
	Reteach		
	—— Reteaching Activity 30–4, TCR 📁	15–20 minutes	ELL, L1
	—— Reading Essentials and Study Guide 30–4, TCR 📁	25–35 minutes	ELL, L1
	—— Take-Home Review Activity 30, TCR 📁	10–15 minutes	All levels
	—— MindJogger Videoquiz, Chapter 30 💿 📼	20–25 minutes	All levels
	Enrich		
	—— Enrichment Activity 30–4, TCR 📁	10–15 minutes	L2, L3
	CLOSE MENU		
	—— Close, TWE, p. 889	10–15 minutes	All levels

See Optional Resources menu on page viii.

Grade _____ Class(es) _____ Date _____ M Tu W Th F

Teacher's Name _____ Date _____

Nixon's Foreign Policy   Section 1 *(pp. 896–900)*

LOCAL OBJECTIVES	TWE—Teacher Wraparound Edition TCR—Teacher Classroom Resources 📁 Blackline Master 🕹 Transparency 💿 CD-ROM ⊙ DVD 📕 Poster 🎵 Music Program 🔊 Audio Program 📼 Videocassette ⊸ Internet Resources

	OBJECTIVES **1.** Explain how Richard Nixon changed U.S. political relations with the Soviet Union and China. **2.** Identify what actions the United States took regarding the Middle East and Latin America.		
	FOCUS MENU	**SUGGESTED TIME RANGES**	**SUGGESTED LEVELS**
	____ Daily Focus Skills Transparency 31–1, TCR 🕹 📁	5–10 minutes	L1
	____ Preteaching Vocabulary, TWE, p. 896	5–10 minutes	All levels
	____ History Online Chapter 31 Overview ⊸	15–20 minutes	All levels
	____ Audio Program Chapter 31 🔊	20–25 minutes	All levels
	TEACH MENU **Guided Practice**		
	____ Time Line Activity, TWE, p. 895	10–15 minutes	All levels
	____ Activity, TWE, p. 897	5–10 minutes	L1
	____ Cooperative Learning Activity, TWE, p. 897	40–60 minutes	L2
	____ Meeting Special Needs, TWE, p. 898	25–35 minutes	L1
	____ Interdisciplinary Connections Activity, TWE, p. 899	20–30 minutes	L2
	____ Graphic Organizer Transparency Strategy and Activity 31, TCR 🕹 📁	15–20 minutes	L2
	Independent Practice		
	____ Guided Reading Activity 31–1, TCR 📁	15–20 minutes	ELL, L1
	____ Reading and Study Skills Foldable, p. 895	10–15 minutes	All levels
	ASSESS MENU **Evaluate**		
	____ Section Quiz 31–1, TCR 📁	10–15 minutes	All levels
	____ Interactive Tutor Self-Assessment CD-ROM 💿	20–30 minutes	All levels
	____ ExamView® Pro Testmaker CD-ROM 💿	15–20 minutes	All levels
	Reteach		
	____ Reteaching Activity 31–1, TCR 📁	15–20 minutes	ELL, L1
	____ Reading Essentials and Study Guide 31–1, TCR 📁	25–35 minutes	ELL, L1
	Enrich		
	____ Enrichment Activity 31–1, TCR 📁	10–15 minutes	L2, L3
	____ Linking Past and Present Activity 31, TCR 📁	15–20 minutes	All levels
	CLOSE MENU ____ Close, TWE, p. 900	10–15 minutes	All levels

See Optional Resources menu on page viii.

Nixon and Watergate

Section 2 (pp. 901–908)

LOCAL OBJECTIVES	TWE—Teacher Wraparound Edition TCR—Teacher Classroom Resources 📁 Blackline Master 🔥 Transparency 💿 CD-ROM 💿 DVD 📕 Poster 🎵 Music Program 🎧 Audio Program 📼 Videocassette 🌐 Internet Resources		
	OBJECTIVES **1.** Describe how Nixon struggled with domestic problems. **2.** Understand how the Watergate scandal affected politics.		
	FOCUS MENU	**SUGGESTED TIME RANGES**	**SUGGESTED LEVELS**
	——— Daily Focus Skills Transparency 31–2, TCR 🔥 📁	5–10 minutes	L1
	——— Preteaching Vocabulary, TWE, p. 901	5–10 minutes	All levels
	——— Audio Program Chapter 31 🎧	20–25 minutes	All levels
	TEACH MENU **Guided Practice**		
	——— Activity, TWE, p. 902	5–10 minutes	L1
	——— Cooperative Learning Activity, TWE, p. 902	40–60 minutes	L1
	——— Meeting Special Needs, TWE, p. 903	25–35 minutes	L1
	——— Interdisciplinary Connections Activity, TWE, p. 904	20–30 minutes	L2
	——— Critical Thinking Activity, TWE, p. 905	20–25 minutes	L3
	——— Extending the Content, TWE, p. 906	5–10 minutes	All levels
	——— Extending the Content, TWE, p. 907	5–10 minutes	All levels
	——— Graphic Organizer Transparencies Strategies and Activities, TCR 🔥 📁	20–25 minutes	All levels
	——— Why It Matters Chapter Transparency Strategy and Activity 31, TCR 🔥 📁	25–30 minutes	All levels
	Independent Practice		
	——— Guided Reading Activity 31–2, TCR 📁	15–20 minutes	ELL, L1
	ASSESS MENU **Evaluate**		
	——— Section Quiz 31–2, TCR 📁	10–15 minutes	All levels
	——— Interactive Tutor Self-Assessment CD-ROM 💿	20–30 minutes	All levels
	——— ExamView® Pro Testmaker CD-ROM 💿	15–20 minutes	All levels
	——— History Online Activity 🌐	15–20 minutes	ELL, L1
	Reteach		
	——— Reteaching Activity 31–2, TCR 📁	15–20 minutes	ELL, L1
	——— Reading Essentials and Study Guide 31–2, TCR 📁	25–35 minutes	L2, L3
	Enrich		
	——— Enrichment Activity 31–2, TCR 📁	10–15 minutes	All levels
	——— Primary Source Reading 31, TCR 📁	20–30 minutes	All levels
	CLOSE MENU		
	——— Close, TWE, p. 908	10–15 minutes	All levels

See Optional Resources menu on page viii.

The Carter Presidency

Section 3 *(pp. 910–914)*

LOCAL OBJECTIVES	TWE—Teacher Wraparound Edition TCR—Teacher Classroom Resources
	📁 Blackline Master 🔦 Transparency 💿 CD-ROM 📀 DVD 🖼 Poster
	🎵 Music Program 🎧 Audio Program 📼 Videocassette 🖱 Internet Resources

OBJECTIVES

1. Explain how President Carter emphasized human rights in foreign policy.
2. Cite the actions Carter took to improve the economy.

FOCUS MENU	SUGGESTED TIME RANGES	SUGGESTED LEVELS
____ Daily Focus Skills Transparency 31–3, TCR 🔦 📁	5–10 minutes	L1
____ Vocabulary PuzzleMaker CD-ROM 💿	5–10 minutes	All levels
____ Audio Program Chapter 31 🎧	20–25 minutes	All levels

TEACH MENU

Guided Practice

____ Activity, TWE, p. 911	5–10 minutes	L2
____ Cooperative Learning Activity, TWE, p. 911	40–60 minutes	L2
____ Meeting Special Needs, TWE, p. 912	25–35 minutes	L1
____ Interdisciplinary Connections Activity, TWE, p. 913	20–30 minutes	ELL, L1
____ Graphic Organizer Transparencies Strategies and Activities, TCR 🔦 📁	20–25 minutes	All levels

Independent Practice

____ Guided Reading Activity 31–3 TCR 📁	15–20 minutes	ELL, L1
____ Vocabulary Activity 31, TCR 📁	20–30 minutes	All levels
____ Chapter Skills Activity 31, TCR 📁	15–20 minutes	L1
____ Critical Thinking Activity 31, TCR 📁	15–20 minutes	L1
____ Geography and History Activity 31, TCR 📁	10–15 minutes	All levels
____ Time Line Activity 31, TCR 📁	15–20 minutes	All levels

ASSESS MENU

Evaluate

____ Section Quiz 31–3, TCR 📁	10–15 minutes	All levels
____ Performance Assessment Activity 31, TCR 📁	25–30 minutes	All levels
____ Interactive Tutor Self-Assessment CD-ROM 💿	20–30 minutes	All levels
____ ExamView® Pro Testmaker CD-ROM 💿	15–20 minutes	All levels

Reteach

____ Reteaching Activity 31–3, TCR 📁	15–20 minutes	ELL, L1
____ Reading Essentials and Study Guide 31–3, TCR 📁	25–35 minutes	ELL, L1
____ Take-Home Review Activity 31, TCR 📁	10–15 minutes	All levels
____ MindJogger Videoquiz, Chapter 31 📀 📼	20–25 minutes	All levels

Enrich

____ Enrichment Activity 31–3, TCR 📁	10–15 minutes	L2, L3

CLOSE MENU

____ Close, TWE, p. 914	10–15 minutes	All levels

See Optional Resources menu on page viii.

Grade _____ Class(es) _____ Date _____ M Tu W Th F

Teacher's Name _____ Date _____

REPRODUCIBLE LESSON PLAN **32–1**

The Reagan Presidency

Section 1 *(pp. 922–926)*

LOCAL OBJECTIVES	TWE—Teacher Wraparound Edition TCR—Teacher Classroom Resources 📁 Blackline Master 🔨 Transparency 💿 CD-ROM 📀 DVD 🪧 Poster 🎵 Music Program 🎧 Audio Program 📼 Videocassette 🔌 Internet Resources		
	OBJECTIVES **1.** Explain how Ronald Reagan implemented supply-side economics. **2.** Describe how Ronald Reagan was active in foreign policy. **3.** Identify changes in the Soviet Union.		
	FOCUS MENU	**SUGGESTED TIME RANGES**	**SUGGESTED LEVELS**
	—— Daily Focus Skills Transparency 32–1, TCR 🔨 📁	5–10 minutes	L1
	—— Preteaching Vocabulary, TWE, p. 922	5–10 minutes	All levels
	—— History Online Chapter 32 Overview 🔌	15–20 minutes	All levels
	—— Audio Program Chapter 32 🎧	20–25 minutes	All levels
	TEACH MENU **Guided Practice**		
	—— Time Line Activity, TWE, p. 921	5–10 minutes	All levels
	—— Activity, TWE, p. 923	5–10 minutes	L2
	—— Cooperative Learning Activity, TWE, p. 923	40–60 minutes	L3
	—— Meeting Special Needs, TWE, p. 924	25–35 minutes	L1
	—— Interdisciplinary Connections Activity, TWE, p. 925	20–30 minutes	L2
	—— Graphic Organizer Transparencies Strategies and Activities, TCR 🔨 📁	20–25 minutes	All levels
	Independent Practice		
	—— Guided Reading Activity 32–1, TCR 📁	15–20 minutes	ELL, L1
	—— Reading and Study Skills Foldable, p. 921	10–15 minutes	All levels
	ASSESS MENU **Evaluate**		
	—— Section Quiz 32–1, TCR 📁	10–15 minutes	All levels
	—— Interactive Tutor Self-Assessment CD-ROM 💿	20–30 minutes	All levels
	—— ExamView® Pro Testmaker CD-ROM 💿	15–20 minutes	All levels
	Reteach		
	—— Reteaching Activity 32–1, TCR 📁	15–20 minutes	ELL, L1
	—— Reading Essentials and Study Guide 32–1, TCR 📁	25–35 minutes	ELL, L1
	Enrich		
	—— Enrichment Activity 32–1, TCR 📁	10–15 minutes	L2, L3
	—— Linking Past and Present Activity 32, TCR 📁	15–20 minutes	All levels
	CLOSE MENU		
	—— Close, TWE, p. 926	10–15 minutes	All levels

See Optional Resources menu on page viii.

The Bush Presidency

Section 2 *(pp. 928–933)*

LOCAL OBJECTIVES	TWE—Teacher Wraparound Edition TCR—Teacher Classroom Resources
	📁 Blackline Master ⚒ Transparency ◉ CD-ROM ◉ DVD 📙 Poster
	🎵 Music Program 🎧 Audio Program 📼 Videocassette 🔌 Internet Resources

	OBJECTIVES
	1. Describe the collapse of the Soviet Union.
	2. Examine how George Bush used the military overseas.
	3. Identify the difficulty that George Bush had domestically.

		SUGGESTED TIME RANGES	SUGGESTED LEVELS
	FOCUS MENU		
	____ Daily Focus Skills Transparency 32–2, TCR ⚒ 📁	5–10 minutes	L1
	____ Preteaching Vocabulary, TWE, p. 928	5–10 minutes	All levels
	____ Audio Program Chapter 32 🎧	20–25 minutes	All levels

	TEACH MENU		
	Guided Practice		
	____ Activity, TWE, p. 929	5–10 minutes	L1
	____ Cooperative Learning Activity, TWE, p. 929	40–60 minutes	L2
	____ Meeting Special Needs, TWE, p. 930	25–35 minutes	L1
	____ Interdisciplinary Connections Activity, TWE, p. 931	20–30 minutes	L2
	____ Critical Thinking Activity, TWE, p. 932	20–25 minutes	L3
	____ Graphic Organizer Transparencies Strategies and Activities, TCR ⚒ 📁	20–25 minutes	All levels
	Independent Practice		
	____ Guided Reading Activity 32–2, TCR 📁	15–20 minutes	ELL, L1

	ASSESS MENU		
	Evaluate		
	____ Section Quiz 32–2, TCR 📁	10–15 minutes	All levels
	____ Interactive Tutor Self-Assessment CD-ROM ◉	20–30 minutes	All levels
	____ ExamView® Pro Testmaker CD-ROM ◉	15–20 minutes	All levels
	Reteach		
	____ Reteaching Activity 32–2, TCR 📁	15–20 minutes	ELL, L1
	____ Reading Essentials and Study Guide 32–2, TCR 📁	25–35 minutes	ELL, L1
	Enrich		
	____ Enrichment Activity 32–2, TCR 📁	10–15 minutes	L2, L3
	____ Primary Source Reading 32, TCR 📁	20–30 minutes	All levels

	CLOSE MENU		
	____ Close, TWE, p. 933	10–15 minutes	All levels

See Optional Resources menu on page viii.

A New Century

Section 3 *(pp. 936–944)*

LOCAL OBJECTIVES	TWE—Teacher Wraparound Edition TCR—Teacher Classroom Resources 📁 Blackline Master 🔨 Transparency 💿 CD-ROM 💿 DVD 📋 Poster 🎵 Music Program 🎧 Audio Program 📼 Videocassette 🌐 Internet Resources		
	OBJECTIVES **1.** Explain why Bill Clinton was impeached by Congress. **2.** Understand why the election of 2000 triggered controversy.		
	FOCUS MENU	**SUGGESTED TIME RANGES**	**SUGGESTED LEVELS**
	—— Daily Focus Skills Transparency 32–3, TCR 🔨 📁	5–10 minutes	L1
	—— Preteaching Vocabulary, TWE, p. 936	5–10 minutes	All levels
	—— Audio Program Chapter 32 🎧	20–25 minutes	All levels
	TEACH MENU **Guided Practice**		
	—— Activity, TWE, p. 937	5–10 minutes	L1
	—— Cooperative Learning Activity, TWE, p. 937	40–60 minutes	L2
	—— Meeting Special Needs, TWE, p. 938	25–35 minutes	L1
	—— Interdisciplinary Connections Activity, TWE, p. 939	20–30 minutes	L3
	—— Critical Thinking Activity, TWE, p. 940	20–25 minutes	L2
	—— Extending the Content, TWE, p. 941	5–10 minutes	All levels
	—— Extending the Content, TWE, p. 942	5–10 minutes	All levels
	—— Extending the Content, TWE, p. 943	5–10 minutes	All levels
	—— Graphic Organizer Transparency Strategy and Activity 32, TCR 🔨 📁	15–20 minutes	L2
	—— American Biographies 📁	25–30 minutes	All levels
	—— American Art and Architecture 🔨 📁	25–30 minutes	All levels
	—— Why It Matters Chapter Transparency Strategy and Activity 32, TCR 🔨 📁	25–30 minutes	All levels
	Independent Practice		
	—— Guided Reading Activity 32–3, TCR 📁	15–20 minutes	ELL, L1
	ASSESS MENU **Evaluate**		
	—— Section Quiz 32–3, TCR 📁	10–15 minutes	All levels
	—— Interactive Tutor Self-Assessment CD-ROM 💿	20–30 minutes	All levels
	—— ExamView® Pro Testmaker CD-ROM 💿	15–20 minutes	All levels
	—— History Online Activity 🌐	15–20 minutes	All levels
	Reteach		
	—— Reteaching Activity 32–3, TCR 📁	15–20 minutes	ELL, L1
	—— Reading Essentials and Study Guide 32–3, TCR 📁	25–35 minutes	ELL, L1
	Enrich		
	—— Enrichment Activity 32–3, TCR 📁	10–15 minutes	L2, L3
	CLOSE MENU		
	—— Close, TWE, p. 944	10–15 minutes	All levels

See Optional Resources menu on page viii.

The War on Terrorism

Section 4 *(pp. 945–951)*

LOCAL OBJECTIVES	TWE—Teacher Wraparound Edition TCR—Teacher Classroom Resources 🗁 Blackline Master ♟ Transparency 💿 CD-ROM ⊙ DVD 📱 Poster 🎵 Music Program 🎧 Audio Program 📼 Videocassette ⬤ Internet Resources		
	OBJECTIVES **1.** Examine how Americans responded to terrorism. **2.** Cite actions the government took to fight terrorism.		
	FOCUS MENU	**SUGGESTED TIME RANGES**	**SUGGESTED LEVELS**
	____ Daily Focus Skills Transparency 32–4, TCR ♟ 🗁	5–10 minutes	L1
	____ Vocabulary PuzzleMaker CD-ROM 💿	5–10 minutes	All levels
	____ Audio Program Chapter 32 🎧	20–25 minutes	All levels
	TEACH MENU **Guided Practice**		
	____ Activity, TWE, p. 946	5–10 minutes	L1
	____ Cooperative Learning Activity, TWE, p. 946	40–60 minutes	L2
	____ Meeting Special Needs, TWE, p. 947	25–35 minutes	L1
	____ Interdisciplinary Connections Activity, TWE, p. 948	20–30 minutes	L3
	____ Critical Thinking Activity, TWE, p. 949	20–25 minutes	L1
	____ Extending the Content, TWE, p. 950	5–10 minutes	All levels
	____ Graphic Organizer Transparencies Strategies and Activities, TCR ♟ 🗁	20–25 minutes	All levels
	Independent Practice		
	____ Guided Reading Activity 32–4 TCR 🗁	15–20 minutes	ELL, L1
	____ Vocabulary Activity 32, TCR 🗁	20–30 minutes	All levels
	____ Chapter Skills Activity 32, TCR 🗁	20–30 minutes	L2, L3
	____ Critical Thinking Activity 32, TCR 🗁	10–15 minutes	L2
	____ Geography and History Activity 32, TCR 🗁	15–20 minutes	All levels
	____ Time Line Activity 32, TCR 🗁	15–20 minutes	All levels
	ASSESS MENU **Evaluate**		
	____ Section Quiz 32–4, TCR 🗁	10–15 minutes	All levels
	____ Performance Assessment Activity 32, TCR 🗁	25–30 minutes	All levels
	____ Interactive Tutor Self-Assessment CD-ROM 💿	20–30 minutes	All levels
	____ ExamView® Pro Testmaker CD-ROM 💿	15–20 minutes	All levels
	Reteach		
	____ Reteaching Activity 32–4, TCR 🗁	15–20 minutes	ELL, L1
	____ Reading Essentials and Study Guide 32–4, TCR 🗁	25–35 minutes	ELL, L1
	____ Take-Home Review Activity 32, TCR 🗁	10–15 minutes	All levels
	____ MindJogger Videoquiz, Chapter 32 ⊙ 📼	20–25 minutes	All levels
	Enrich		
	____ Enrichment Activity 32–4, TCR 🗁	10–15 minutes	L2, L3
	CLOSE MENU		
	____ Close, TWE, p. 951	10–15 minutes	All levels

See Optional Resources menu on page viii.

DATE DUE

GAYLORD			PRINTED IN U.S.A.